Occasional Papers Series
No. 8

Amatxi, Amuma, Amona

Writings in Honor of Basque Women

Edited by

Linda White and Cameron Watson

Center for Basque Studies
University of Nevada, Reno

© 2017 Center for Basque Studies

Occasional Papers Series, No. 8

Center for Basque Studies

University of Nevada, Reno

Reno, Nevada

Originally published in 2003 by the Center for Basque Studies

Book and cover design by Juan San Martin

Cover photo courtesy of Juan San Martin

ISBN: 978-1-935709-87-9

Contents

Introduction

Any anthology necessarily suffers from the question of classification. How should the articles be presented? According to which criteria should they be arranged? Classification is quite obviously an exercise in power that requires the utmost consideration. One potential classification scheme would have been to organize the articles in historical sequence, thereby presenting a series of individual experiences throughout history with the aim of tracing similarities or trends that might represent Basque women through time. Another form of categorization might have been geographical; that is, one based on differentiating the Old World experience from New World practices. Again, the focus here might have been to suggest patterns of this experience traversing oceans and continents. Ultimately, however, we hope that the following classification scheme will serve to highlight these questions *defacto*. Indeed, we ask of the reader only that they consider the multiple possibilities afforded by coming into contact with a diverse range of personal histories and experiences.

Many works that deal solely with theory and statistics, while offering important and useful information, overlook the individual experience. This is true even of those works that rely on individual interviews to present a universal picture of a group experience. We therefore suggest here that, in the first instance, what counts is the individual experience of the women concerned. Secondly, however, we would also point out that there are parallels, both subtle and more obvious, between the experiences of the women encountered in this anthology.

We argue here that identity, whether gender or culture-based, does matter. Indeed in an increasingly similar world of global trends and lifestyles people are turning to elements of their own identity that help them maintain that individuality, even, ironically, if that means identification with particular groups.

Basque women have played strong, diverse roles within their cultures, both that of the Basque country and that of the Basque community spread throughout the world. The voices that have contributed to this volume pay homage to those roles in different ways. We begin with two works of fiction by Basque-American writers, each recounting a tale of childhood shaped by Basque grandmothers. The other writings are loosely arranged to carry us from fiction to personal recollection and finally to the purely academic.

Martin Etchart was born and raised in Arizona. His Basque grandmother and grandfather were from Urepel, France, where many of his relatives still reside. Etchart obtained his Ph.D. in 2002 in Creative Writing with an emphasis in Basque studies, and he currently teaches literature and the writing of fiction at Phoenix College in Phoenix, Arizona.

Etchart's "Amatxi" captures a day of transition in the life of a thirteen-year-old Basque-American boy who learns about love and hope and the power of family while helping his grandmother prepare Easter dinner. Etchart's personal memories of his own childhood flavor his fiction with an authenticity that will resonate with all those who have witnessed the generational transition from immigrant to American-born in their own families.

There are several Basque words sprinkled throughout Etchart's story. For those who are interested, they are listed here with their English translations. To translate them within the story would destroy the rhythm of the fiction.

oilaskoa arno zurian	chicken in white wine
lamia	mythological creature
Mamu	mythological creature used to frighten naughty children
sorgina	witch
gaixua	dear little one
ene eskuak	my hands
orain	now
ba	yes
ez	no
aita	father
neskak	girls
badikzu euskera	you know Basque (phonetic representation of dialect)
puzkat bakarrik	only a little
Euskal Herria	the Basque Country
Zer?	What?
Polita	pretty
Ttanta	aunt (borrowed from French
Isilik	be quiet
Aiyiyama	oh my goodness
Ama	mother
arno gorria	red wine
gizona	man
txin, txin	a traditional toast
Joan	go
"Uso zuria"	white dove (a song title)

Maria Davis Denzler is a second-generation native Nevadan, descended from Basque immigrants who helped build Nevada's ranching industry in the early part of the twentieth century. She currently works as a non-fiction feature writer for *Nevada Magazine,* and is also writing a novel about water in the West. She earned a degree in biology before becoming a full-time writer, and has worked for organizations such as the U.S. Forest Service, the Nature Conservancy, the Walker Lake Working Group, and the Grace Dangberg Foundation.

Denzler's fascination with the Great Basin and its inhabitants began as a child with forays out into the sagebrush desert near the mining town of Battle Mountain, Nevada, where she and her sister spent endless days searching for lizards, coyotes and adventure. She currently resides in Reno with her husband, Mark, two children, and Great Pyrenees dog, Ocho.

Maria Denzler's "Into the Dark" is a haunting, lyric tale of the presence of an owl that links grandmother to granddaughter. The characters in the story are once again immigrant grandparents and Americanized desdendants. The recurring appearance of the owl links the past to the present as each woman — grandmother, mother, and daughter — feels the presence of the mysterious bird in their lives. The events of "Into the Dark" transpire over the course of sixty-five years, and yet we feel the connection through the generations as if we had lived those years ourselves.Denzler's characters speak a mixture of Spanish and Basque, a situation that was very common among immigrants. She reveals this through words such as *en tiempo* 'soon' and *bastante* 'enough,' while Jose calls his wife by the Basque world for mother, Ama. The names of her grandparents are spelled Jose and Marichu, without diacriticals and before the advent of Basque Language Academy spelling conventions that would express Marichu as Maritxu today. These spellings are true to the early Basque reality in America, since the immigrants arrived before Unified Basque was created. The constant presence of English also contributes to the loss of diacriticals, as in Jose and Maria, since such marks are never used in English names. Bianka Vidonja Balanzategui is a professional historian from North Queensland, Australia. A trained secondary school teacher, she is currently doing substitute teaching in both primary and secondary schools while completing her Ph.D. at James Cook University in Townsland, Queensland. Inspired by her father's experience as a displaced immigrant sent to cut sugar cane on arrival in Australia, she wrote *Gentlemen of the Flashing Blade.* This book inspired a documentary of the same name that later appeared on Australian TV. She has also published in the *Journal of the Society of Basque Studies in America* (2001) about the history of a Basque fronton in Trebonne, Queensland. Her chief research interests are the Australian sugar industry and European migration to Australia, especially that pertaining to the Basques and post-World War Two displaced persons.

In "Basking in a Different Sun: The Story of Conchi Mendiolea," Vidonja Balanzategui brings to bear her personal knowledge of the migrant experience in North Queensland, Australia in an article exploring the life of Conchi Mendiolea. Born in Lekeitio, Bizkaia, in 1944, Concepción Arrasate married Australia-born Juan Mendiolea while he was visiting the old country. Vidonja Balanzategui traces the hardship faced by Conchi during her early years in Australia and the numerous cultural obstacles she had to overcome in order to truly settle in a foreign land. While successfully adapting to the new country, she also retained a strong sense of her natal identity and has been a focal point of the Basque-Australian community in the Herbert River district of Queensland. Vidonja Balanzategui demonstrates how creative pursuits have served to express Conchi's thoughts and feelings in her later years about her multiple identities: woman, wife, mother, Basque, and Australian.

Pianist Estibaliz Gastesi, a native of the Basque Country, has performed throughout Europe and the United States, both solo and in duo with her husband Márcio Bezerra. She graduated with honors from Bilbao's Arriaga Conservatory, subsequently moving to the United States where she received a Doctor of Musical Arts Degree from the University of Arizona in 1998. Dr. Gastesi is an active ethnomusicologist who has published widely and attended international conferences in this field. For example, at the 36th World Conference of the International Council of Traditional Music she presented a paper dealing with the music of Basque immigrants in the United States.

Gastesi's "Emiliana de Zubeldia" traces the life and work of the Basque pianist and composer. In a personal story marked by professional success and private upheaval, Gastesi demonstrates how Zubeldia maintained a strong Basque identity, despite constantly traveling the world to play at the foremost concert venues. Zubeldia spent most of her life away from her birthplace. She ultimately settled in Mexico where, after an accident that cut short her performing career, she dedicated the rest of her life to teaching, directing her university choir, and providing resources to enable students from humble backgrounds to study music. Gastesi concludes that Zubeldia used music as a means of maintaining and expressing both her Basque and her diaspora identity.

Freelance writer Rachel Bard holds a B.A. in Spanish and an M.A. in Spanish History from the University of Washington. She has also studied at the University of Navarre in Pamplona. She has worked in public relations and advertising, as well as teaching journalism at Tacoma Community College in Washington. She is the author of nine books including *Navarre: The Durable Kingdom* (1982) *and Queen without a Country* (2001). Her articles include "The Decline of a Basque State in France: Basse Navarre, 1512 — 1789" *in Anglo-Ameri-*

can Contributions to Basque Studies: Essays in Honor of Jon Bilbao (1977) and "Aimery Picaud and the Basques: Selections from the Pilgrim's Guide to Santiago de Compostela" in *Essays in Basque Social Anthropology and History* (1989).

Bard's "Berengaria of Navarre: Medieval Role Model," attempts to rescue a little-known, but important, twelfth-century Basque female figure from the depths of history. Queen Berengaria of Navarre, argues Bard, provides an early example of a strong and determined woman who succeeded in charting her own life in a male-dominated world while embodying what many consider typically Basque cultural values: tenacity, self-respect and probity. However, Berengaria's legacy has been all but forgotten, and Bard speculates that in many ways, she was a ruler ahead of her time. That said, as the article concludes, in the French city of Le Mans, where she spent her last days, her good works and charity are remembered to this day.

M.E.R. "Maggi" Nicholson is a cultural anthropologist who teaches at the Emeritus College of the College of Marin in California. In 1979 she became an adjunct professor with the Center for Basque Studies and has published five articles about her research carried out in the Basque Country. Her conversations with Claire Noblia have spanned more than a decade.

Nicholson's "Becoming Basque: The *Euskarapen* of Raymonde and Claire Noblia" is the true story of a mother and daughter who were born in Iparralde, the northern Basque country, but were not raised as Basques. Only later in life did they each separately make a commitment to embrace the Basque language and culture as their own. Although they lived in Europe and West Africa, their search for Basque identity has much in common with similar odysseys of second and third-generation Basque-American women who expend tremendous energies in their efforts to maintain Basqueness in their lives and in the lives of their families.

In her later years, Raymonde investigated the genealogies of her family and that of her husband. Only then did she discover that she had forty-seven Basque ancestors through the line of her maternal grandmother. Her daughter Claire started an *ikastola* or Basque-language elementary school, and later initiated the formation of a parents' association, called *Seaska* 'Cradle,' to augment the school, hire teachers, and start pre-school classes. In 1999, Seaska celebrated its thirtieth anniversary and was offering classes from pre-school through high school in Iparralde.

David Río is Professor of American Literature at the University of the Basque Country in Vitoria-Gasteiz. He is the author of *El proceso de la violencia en la narrativa de Robert Venn Warren* (1995) and *Robert Laxalt: La voz de los vascos en la literatura norteamericana* (2002). He has also published several articles on Basque-American writers in various American and European journals.

Río's "Monique Laxalt: A Literary Interpreter for the New Generations of Basque-Americans" not only provides keen insight on Monique Laxalt but explores her intimate struggles with the different facets of her own identity, both as she expressed them in the poetic novel *The Deep Blue Memory* (1993) and from his own unique perspective as a specialist in the writings of the Laxalt family. Monique Laxalt writes as a woman and as a third-generation Basque-American, using both perspectives to demonstrate the conflict she has experienced between the process of Americanization of her family and the loyalty she feels toward ethnic ties that seem more distant every generation.

Río follows her personal journey as she left her law pratice in 1990 to dedicate herself to writing the novel and to exploring her Basque heritage in the light of her upbringing within American society. Río's analysis of her novel is accomplished as a parallel to his commentary on her personal struggle to maintain her identity as an individual while respecting the reputation and notoriety of her famous family.

Gloria Totoricagüena teaches and researches at the Center for Basque Studies in the University of Nevada, Reno. She earned her Bachelor's Degree in Political Science from Boise State University in 1986. She went on to obtain a Specialist Degree in Latin American Politics and Economic Development from the Universidad de la República (Montevideo, Uruguay) in 1987, then a Master's Degree in Education from Boise State University in 1989, and finally her Ph.D. in Comparative Politics at the London School of Economics and Political Science in 2000. She is a Project Director for "Urazandi: Basques across the Seas," a fifteen-book series exploring Basque migration, identity maintenance, and transnational networks. She is also the Series Director of Basques in the United States for the Internet version of the *Enciclopedia General Ilustrada del País Vasco,* for the Editorial Auñamendi of Donostia-San Sebastián. Dr. Totoricagüena has published widely and her Ph.D. thesis will soon be available in book form from the University of Nevada Press. She has also received numerous awards for teaching excellence and regularly presents her research at international conferences. Her research interests include: a comparison of the Basque diaspora experience with those of other ethnic diasporas such as those of the Greek, Italian, Armenian, and Irish; collecting oral histories from Basque emigrants to the United States; transnational identities and globalization; and analyzing Basque Government policies and relationships with their diasporic communities around the world.

Totoricagüena's "Interconnected Disconnectedness: How Diaspora Basque Women Maintain Ethnic Identity," offers a cross-continental macro-analysis of how women of the Basque diaspora from Argentina to Australia, by way of Belgium, maintain their ethnic identity despite residing in very different countries. The article also attempts to recover the hidden figure of the Basque woman — either omitted entirely (as women) or subsumed within the categories of French or Spanish — in studies of migration. Totoricagüena's analysis, among other conclusions, challenges the often perceived notion that women are the primary "cultural carriers" of an ethnic group. She also finds that, while women of the Basque diaspora value Euskara (the Basque language), they do not believe it an absolutely necessary component of defining an individual's Basque identity. That said, they do in general, and through a myriad of ways, feel it important to maintain and promote a sense of "Basqueness." Furthermore, contends Totoricagüena, this (often personal) commitment to cultural preservation tends to outweigh any specific political involvement in Basque affairs.

Maite Nuñez-Betelu, originally from Donostia, Gipuzkoa, has lived and worked in the United States since 1993. She is currently Assistant Professor of Spanish at the University of Missouri-St. Louis. She earned her Bachelor's Degree from the University of the Basque Country (Gasteiz, Araba), a Master's Degree in Comparative Literature from West Virginia University, and a Ph.D. from the University of Missouri-Columbia in 2001, with a dissertation entitled "Género y construcción nacional en las escritoras vascas" (Gender and National Construction in Basque Women Writers). The annotated bibliography attached to this dissertation was subsequently accepted for publication by the Mellen Press.

In "Euskadi-Venezuela: Natural Poetic Rapprochement," Nuñez-Betelu considers the work of the exiled Basque poet, Balendiñe Albizu, from an ecofeminist perspective, that is to say, from the way in which Albizu employs nature, and especially landscape, in her poetry to challenge traditional male concepts of the world. Nuñez-Betelu argues that, as a post-Spanish Civil War Basque political refugee in Venezuela, Albizu found her poetic voice in the new world by looking back to the old and gradually integrating the two. Albizu maintained her Basque identity through a strong personal political commitment to the Basque Country, as expressed in her poetry. Added to the political struggle of the Basque Country to maintain its identity, she believed a branch of Basque culture could be nurtured in the new world. Ultimately, she uses the metaphor of nature — naturally free of the impositions of man — to argue for Basque independence. This independence is a state of mind that effortlessly crosses the ocean uniting, rather than dividing, Euskadi and Venezuela, or the Basque Country and its diaspora.

Cameron Watson received a B.A. Honours Degree in History from the University of Ulster, Coleraine, Northern Ireland (1988), and thereafter an M.A. in History (1992) and a Ph.D. in Basque Studies (History) (1996), both from the University of Nevada, Reno. He was Assistant Professor of History at the University of Nevada, Reno from 1996 to 1999 and currently teaches in the Basque Country, both at Mondragón University and for the University Studies Abroad Consortium (USAC) program at the University of the Basque Country. He is an Adjunct Professor with the Center for Basque Studies at the University of Nevada, Reno.

He has published "Ethnic Conflict and the League of Nations: The Case of Transylvania, 1918-1940" (1994), "Folklore and Basque Nationalism: Language, Myth, Reality" (1996), "Imagining ETA," in *Basque Politics and Nationalism on the Eve of the Millennium* (1999), and (with Pauliina Raento), "Gernika, Guernica, *Guernica}* Contested Meanings of a Basque Place" (2000). He has also written a textbook, *Modern Basque History, Eighteenth Century to the Present* (Center for Basque Studies, University of Nevada, Reno, 2002). His research interests include Basque and Iberian culture and history, Celtic identity and nationalism, modern European history and the impact of modernity on European society, nationalism and the construction of cultural identity, and ethnic conflict and political violence.

In "The Tragedy of Yoyes," Watson traces the life, and tragic death, of one of the most enigmatic figures of recent Basque history: the ETA activist María Dolores González Katarain or "Yoyes." He argues that the figure of Yoyes has been appropriated by various political agendas to obscure what she really believed and did. He further contends that her life and death encapsulate the drama and tragedy of the recent Basque political experience. The article is thus an attempt to reconsider the experience of Yoyes with regard to her own role as a prominent woman in contemporary Basque political history and the legacy that her tragic death subsequently bequeathed this same history.

Linda White spent fifteen years studying Euskara in preparation for delving into Basque literature in order to obtain a Ph.D. in Basque Studies (Language and Literature) in 1996. She has been with the Center for Basque Studies at the University of Nevada, Reno since 1981, during which time she co-authored the *English-Basque Dictionary* (1990) and the *Basque-English English-Basque Dictionary* (1992), both with Gorka Aulestia. Her dissertation *Emakumeen hitzak euskaraz: Basque Women Writers of the Twentieth Century* debunked the myth that only ten or twenty women had ever written and published in Euskara and provided the English-speaking world with the first history of women's contributions to Basque literature. She has also translated several books by and about Basques, co-edited three earlier volumes of essays, and written many articles about Basque literature. She teaches Euskara at the University of Nevada, Reno and is preparing a self-teaching textbook for English speakers who wish to learn the language but have no access to classroom instruction.

White's "From the Outside Looking In: Basque Women

Writers Urretabizkaia, Mintegi, and Oñederra" explores the work of three women who write in Euskara at different points in the recent history of Basque literature. In addition to the literary perspective, White addresses different issues that figure prominently in the reality of Basque women writers, including attitudes toward feminism, personal and political ramifications of choosing to write in Euskara, and the place of the woman writer in the Basque literary community during the latter twentieth century.

Arantxa Urretabizkaia broke critical ground for women writing in the second half of the twentieth century with her novella *Zergatik, Panpox?* (1979), demonstrating that the lyrical vein so prominent throughout serious Basque narrative is well within the grasp of female artists as well. Laura Mintegi conjoined the themes of love and nationalism in *Nerea eta biok* (1994), producing a novel that was not well accepted in Basque literary circles but says a great deal about the place of woman in Basque society at the time it was published. Lourdes Oñederra's *Eta emakumeari sugeak esan zion* (1999) appeared only five years after Mintegi's book, but the generational gap between these books feels as great as that between Mintegi's and Urretabizkaia's novels. All three, however, turn their backs on feminism as an issue and portray instead concerns and perspectives that are more important to Basque women.

White's personal reflections from the point of view of a non-Basque observing the lives of Basque women in Euskal Herria closes the volume by acknowledging that only those who have lived as Basque women can truly understand the depth and breadth of that experience.

We began by explaining that we have organized this volume to emphasize the individual experience of the women concerned. We conclude by acknowledging that such experience has many layers, and the several authors who have collaborated to make this volume possible have each brought their own perspective to the explorations and homages presented herein. Our desire was to present the reader with options beyond the purely academic in order to reflect more than one layer of experience from varying perspectives. We hope you agree that we have succeeded.

Linda White and Cameron Watson

Amatxi

Martin Etchart

The day after my 13th birthday was Easter and I was stuck sitting at Amatxi's wooden kitchen table cleaning green beans.

The odor of garlic hung thick in the air and pots of *oilaskoa arno zurian* bubbled on the stove as I snapped the beans into a copper pot that sat on a cherry red stain in the shape of a swooping hawk. Clinging to the tip of the hawk's tail was a pea green *lamia,* legs splayed as he flew through the air with a cluster of mustard flowers in his hand. Like shapes in passing clouds, the stained images spread across the table's gouged surface. The *Mamu* and a *sorgina* lurked amid three-legged cows and winged pigs. And a princess, only visible by the tip of her pointy hat, lived in a gravy castle that rose to become a Kool-aid grape river flowing into the mouth of a giant. There were knights and dragons on Amatxi's table, and even the head of George Washington riding on the back of a three-humped grease camel. But I didn't care about any of the creatures spread out in front of me that day. I had my mind on other things, not the least being my twin five-year-old brothers, Mathieu and Ferdinand, who I could see through the kitchen window, laughing as they chased lambs around the farmyard.

I glared as Mathieu caught one of the lambs around the neck and Ferdinand ran up to kiss it on the head. It wasn't fair, me having to work and them playing. I was the one who had shown my brothers how to catch a lamb around the neck and where the ladder leading up to the hayloft was and how you could swing from the rope there to land in a mountain of wool. Mathieu kissed the lamb on the head, too, before letting it go, and I meanly envisioned the trembling lower lips I could cause if I got my brothers alone and informed them that that same lamb they were playing with would be on the Easter dinner table next year. And maybe I'd even tell my brothers the truth about Dad moving out. How he wasn't just going on "a little vacation" and that things wouldn't be "just the same" as my parents had told them.

"You break off sharp at ends, *gaixua*" Amatxi said as she looked over her shoulder at me from where she was cutting slits in a leg of lamb and stuffing in cloves of garlic. "Quick like breaking chicken neck."

"That's a nice thought," I said and pretended I was breaking a neck, only it wasn't a chicken's.

Mom had dropped me and my brothers off at my grandparents' farm early that morning. We always had Easter dinner there with all of my aunts and uncles and cousins. And usually I enjoyed it. Easter at Amatxi and Aitatxi's was like being in the middle of a cyclone where everything is sound and movement: aunts and uncles talking and drinking, and cousins singing and laughing, and everyone passing plates over their heads, and pieces of stories — some new, mostly old — flying through the air. And in the middle of the chaos, loving every moment of it, was me.

My family never arrived at the farm until two or three, an hour before dinner. Only this year, Mom drove me and my brothers out right after breakfast, and on the way announced that now that I was thirteen, I was old enough to help Amatxi with Easter dinner.

"But that's girl stuff," I said.

"You sound like your father," Mom said.

Dad and Mom weren't going to be at Easter dinner. While

we were out of the house, my parents planned to move Dad's stuff into his new apartment.

"She needs help, Michael," Mom said. "She's eighty-eight."

Eighty-eight. I couldn't even do that many sit-ups, and I'd tried.

"When you get done with beans," Amatxi said, "you maybe can help me with peeling potatoes, *gaixua!*"

"Don't call me that," I said, a little louder than I'd meant to as I was thinking about Dad, wondering if he would take with him the plaster cast of my hands I made for him in kindergarten, the one with the words *ene eskuak,* or leave it behind along with the picture of the two of us from the summer before, at the edge of the lake, me holding a bass in my hands — the first fish I ever caught — and grinning with Dad beside me.

"You're right," Amatxi said as she laid the leg of lamb into a pan and then went to wash her hands in the sink. "You too old to be a 'dear little one' anymore. You man *orain.*"

"Now you're talking," I said as I stopped snapping green beans and bit into the sourdough toast Amatxi had made for me.

"It's time you start looking for a wife."

Crumbs of toast fell out of my mouth. Amatxi's back was to me, her compact frame silhouetted in the light coming from the window she was looking out, so I couldn't see if there was a trace of a smile on her face to tell me she was joking.

"*Ba,* it good time to think on marriage for you."

The water was running in the sink, splashing over her hands, and I wondered what could have possibly turned her mind from cooking to marriage? What did she see through that window? My little brothers playing? Aitatxi feeding the chickens? Was she thinking about all the years she'd been with him? Or was she thinking about her son, my father, and what was happening in his marriage? And what was happening between him and Mom? They didn't look like they were mad at each other. Dad did seem to be at work a lot, but we went to Disneyland a month earlier. Dad laughed on the roller coaster. Mom ate cotton candy with her hands. But they didn't talk in the car on the drive over, and my parents always talked in the car—about road signs that didn't make sense, and past trips they'd been on, and vacations yet to come. But this time, the car was silent. Still, I caught them kissing in the kitchen before dinner last week. I told them to stop. It was embarrassing. And they had.

What changed? Why was Dad moving out? And what did that mean? Forever? No one had bothered to explain the details to me. All I knew was that waking up without my father there was something I never imagined I would have to do.

"I'm thirteen," I said to Amatxi, thinking that maybe she'd forgotten my age. Like the time she forgot that Oscar Mayer didn't make blood sausage.

I attributed Amatxi's lapse in memory to her age.

And, as if reading my mind, Amatxi said, "After you get married, age it no matter. You have babies until you no can have anymore. He get old, you get old. You both start to shrink, like you becoming children again."

Amatxi didn't even turn around as she shut off the water and gave the mound of sourdough bread dough sitting on the counter a firm slap as if startling it to life.

"I'm not even in high school yet."

"Thirteen is perfect age to start looking. You wait any longer, the good wives all gone."

Amatxi tilted her head back in concentration as she kneaded the sourdough.

"She must have a big heart."

"So she can love me a lot?" I said with a smile, still hoping this conversation was a joke and Amatxi wasn't serious about finding me a wife.

"Ez so she can forgive you a lot."

"Maybe I should talk to Aitatxi about this," I said, thinking I could sidetrack her. But Amatxi was on a mission.

"Ha," Amatxi said as she turned around to face me. "Why you talk to men about women? They know nothing."

"He knew enough to marry you."

"I marry him."

I decided to turn to the offensive.

"Well then, how old were you?"

"I eleven years old."

"You got married when you were eleven?"

"Ez I see Aitatxi for first time when I eleven. Was in church. He just a boy. All nose even then." "What did he say to you?"

"He say, 'Would you like glass of *arno zuria?*"

"He asked you if you wanted wine in church?"

"What church? We at picnic."

"But you were only eleven?"

"You no listening, *gaixua.*"

"Yeah I am," I said. "You just said the first time you met Aitatxi was in church — "

"I no say 'met.' I say 'see.' Aitatxi very shy. He no talk to me until I seventeen."

"He waited six years to talk to you?'

"Aitatxi a very patient man. I no so patient. I need to start having babies so I — "

"Oh my God," I said. "I don't want to hear anything about sex."

"I no talking about sex. I talking about pushing a sheep through keyhole. Believe me you, that and sex they nothing the same."

"You ever hear of the phrase, 'oversharing,' Amatxi?"

"We family, you no can over share with family. Under share, *ba,* we do that all the time."

Amatxi walked over and pointed to a stain on the wood table. When I tilted my head to the right, I saw that it was in the shape of cow's head.

"You see this?"

"Yeah."

"You know what is?"

"A wine stain."

"*Ba,* we drink plenty of wine after your *aita* born right here."

"Dad was born on this table?"

"All my children born here."

I dropped the piece of sourdough toast I was holding as I pictured my father popping out of Amatxi to lie next to a loaf of sourdough bread, a length of hard salami, and a jug of red wine.

"I'm not hungry anymore."

Amatxi took a seat at the table.

"There any pretty *neskak* at school you like?"

"*Neskak?*"

"Girls. *Badikzu euskera*"

"Puzkat bakarrik, Amatxi."

"Maybe we send you to *Euskal Herria.* You learn *Euskera* and find you a Basque wife. *Ba,* I think that — "

"Don't you need to keep cooking? Everyone's going to be hungry when they get here!"

"They time, *gaixua.* This important."

"But what if I don't want to get married?"

"Zer? How come you say this?"

I ran my eyes over the stains of the table. For the first time I realized that for Amatxi every stain had a different story than the one I made up and attached to it. Like pictures in a photo alburn, the stains captured moments of Amatxi and Aitatxi's lives together.

"Dad and Mom aren't coming today," I said.

"I know this."

"Do you think Dad will ever come here again? I mean with Mom?"

"How I know?"

"Didn't he tell you anything?

Amatxi sighed as she pushed back her chair.

"You open stove."

I pulled open the stove door as Amatxi picked up the pan with the lamb in it and slid it inside.

"I ever tell you story of window?" Amatxi said as she set a bowl of unpeeled potatoes in the middle of the table and handed me a knife.

"Is this like the story of Mari that Aitatxi told me? About how Mari flies through the air in a ball of fire? And how she comes down on you like a thunderstorm and hits you over the head with hailstones."

"He confused," Amatxi said. "Aitatxi not describing Mari but old girlfriend. I seen her. *Aiyiyama,* she have the face like a cow that not been milked in a month. *Ez* I tell story of my best friend from Urepel, Agatha Carategia."

I started peeling potatoes as Amatxi began, "Agatha Carategia, she like a flower on the side of mountain. She have the hair dark that move like a tail when she run, and eyebrows that were so nice and full."

"She sounds more like a squirrel than a flower," I said. "She no squirrel. She very *polita*"

"Did she have a mustache like *Ttanta* Theresea?" I said

"Isilik" Amatxi said. "Now then, we grow up next to each other. We share everything. Agatha was who I first tell about your Aitatxi and how he try and kiss me under the apple tree."

"I thought you said Aitatxi was shy."

"Okay, I kiss him. Now stop you talking in my story."

Amatxi took the potatoes I peeled and cut them into quarters the long way and placed the potatoes around the already cooking lamb. They sizzled as they hit the juice in the pan. Then she had me salt and pepper both the lamb and potatoes before reshutting the oven door.

"Where am I?" Amatxi said.

"The flower girl and kissing," I said.

"Ba, and I was the one whose shoulder Agatha cry on when her parents tell her she going to have to marry Roberto Igaldo. 'His head is like a cured ham,' Agatha say to me. And she right. I seen him in town. He look like a lump of dough God forget to mold. His hands, *aiyiyama,* they fingers as big as

poor Agatha's wrists. What he do to her when they on honey-moon, I no like to —."

"Amatxi."

"Fine. So, I come up with the idea of her going to America with Aitatxi and me after we married. 'You can marry anyone you want there,' I tell her. She very happy. Then all we have to do is wait for March when wedding planned for."

Amatxi scooped out two bowls of *oilaskoa arno zurian*. She set one in front of me and I smiled as the smell of the chicken cooked in white wine filled my head.

"It hot, *gaixua*" Amatxi said.

But I didn't care. I scooped the steaming chicken into my mouth. "See, no so bad helping Amatxi in kitchen." "Can I have some more?"

"Ez, you keep some space inside for dinner," Amatxi said as she picked up a chicken leg from her bowl and began to pull the meat off it in strips as she ate it. "After we married, Aitatxi and me plan to go by boat to New York. We wait for honeymoon over and go by May first. Agatha, she so excited she no can hardly wait to leave. But she no tell no one about her going. She still play like going to marry Roberto. They go on dates with chaperone. They walk together, sit by the stream. And Agatha she tell me how dull he is. 'All he talks about are his sheep.' And I tell her that in New York they lots of men who never even seen sheep except on dinner plate. We talk and planned. And then come day for us to go. The night before we to leave, I sneak over to Agatha's house. The windows they all dark except for kitchen. I go there thinking to knock and make sure Agatha ready. But when I look through window, all I see is flicker from fireplace. I move to go and light from moon fall through window and I see them. They sitting there in front of the fire."

"Who?" I said as I leaned forward with my elbows on the table and my head cradled between my hands.

"Agatha and Roberto," Amatxi said. "They holding hands. Or she holding his hand. In moonlight, I see her lips moving, but I no hear what she say. I think she telling Roberto she no can marry him and how she going to America. But then she kiss him, on the forehead, soft, like *ama* kisses her baby. And she run her little hand over his lumpy ham head and I no understand. I seen them together. I hear what she tell me. This no make sense. Next day, your aitatxi and me we go on boat. Agatha she marry Roberto. They have eight kids. All with ham heads. *Aiyiyama*"

Amatxi pushed back her chair and picked up the empty bowls from the table. She laid them in the sink and again turned to the sourdough sitting on the counter.

"Michael, you get me pan out of cupboard for bread," Amatxi said. "It getting late. We have to hurry."

"Wait a minute," I said, my chair grating over the wooden floor as I stood up. "That's it?"

Amatxi looked at me, *"Ba,* that window story."

"That's a lousy story. And what has that got to do with Mom and Dad?"

Amatxi didn't answer me, but instead went to the cabinet above the stove and opened it. She took down a bottle of red wine and two glasses.

"You like *arno gorria?"*

"I'm not allowed to have wine."

"You *gizona* now, you can have — but just *puzkat"*

"Cool," I said.

"But you no going to like," Amatxi said as she poured wine into the two glasses. One she filled to the top, the other only a quarter of the way. She handed me the full glass.

I grinned as I took it.

"*Txin, txin*" Amatxi said as she raised her glass to clink against mine.

"*Txin, txin*" I said and took a gulp of wine which I then spit out over the table.

I grabbed a napkin and wiped off my tongue.

"That's disgusting," I said. The sour taste of the wine seemed to make my tongue swell.

Amatxi took a sip from her glass and smiled.

"What you think it going to taste like?"

"Not like vinegar," I said. "Something good like grape juice."

"I tell you you no going to like."

"I thought you were just saying that to keep me from drinking it."

"You think it look like grape juice?" Amatxi said.

"It does."

"That because you only see through glass. You no understand because you no inside glass."

"I don't think I'd fit," I said as I pushed the glass of wine further away from me.

"*Ba,* and I no fit in that kitchen with Agatha and Roberto."

"Are we back to the story?"

"Agatha and Roberto, they like that wine. Agatha, she tell me about her and Roberto, and I see them together, but I still no know because she inside glass like wine. Wine I no can taste — not ever. Is all their own."

"I don't get it."

"I see my son and his wife. You see your parents. But what their marriage is, only they can know. We can only look."

"So they'll get back together?" I said.

"No one likes to throw away wine," Amatxi said. "Even if sometimes it taste a little sour."

I was about to point out to Amatxi that you could always just go to the store and buy a new bottle of wine when I saw my Uncle Fred's red pickup pull up outside. My cousin Dominic jumped out of the passenger side and came rushing through the kitchen doorway.

"Come on, Michael, let's climb the hayloft."

I looked to Amatxi who said, *"Joan."*

"Thanks Amatxi," I said, and as I got up, I noticed the red dots of the wine I had spit out scattered over the table. My first taste of wine stained the wood, the splatters connecting that moment to all the moments that had come before.

I ran after Dominic.

That Easter, at Amatxi's insistence, I was seated at the adult table instead of the kids'. My cousin, Henri, who was seventeen, glared at me from where he was stuck between Ferdinand and Mathieu.

And as I sat amid my aunts and uncles, I was offered my second glass of wine, which I accepted but left untasted next to my plate.

Then, as Amatxi was clearing the plates for dessert, Mom and Dad appeared in the doorway. For a moment the room went silent. They were holding hands and looked embarrassed, like kids on a first date. Then my dad said, "I hope there's at least some wine left for us."

And Amatxi said, "We save best for you."

And then everyone laughed and I was caught up in the

cyclone of my family as my Uncle Fred started singing "Uso Zuria" and everyone threw their arms around each others' shoulders and sang along.

Across the table my father was smiling with one arm holding onto Amatxi and the other clasped firmly around my mother. Then Aitatxi raised his glass for a toast, and I raised mine along with all the others. And when we clinked our glasses to *"txin, txin"* the wine caught the light coming through the window. And in that light I saw how the wine looked ruby red in some glasses and royal purple in others and even indigo blue in a few, with a taste both bitter and sweet.

Into the Dark

Maria Davis Denzler

1931 — Martin Ranch, Nevada desert

"Don't kill the owls, *compadre*" said Pete urgently to the ranch foreman. "Bad luck killing those birds. It's why your girl is so sick."

Jose ran a callused hand through his thick Basque hair before replying.

"Those goddamn birds, I need to get rid of them. I lose two or three chicks every other day, lately."

He squinted his eyes and looked out the window past the hen house, beyond the cottonwoods framing the creek, and scanned the mountains to the west. The snow was deep now, the summer range impassable this time of year. His eyes moved back and forth across the range of peaks that he would see again in a few months when the sheep were moved up into the high country. His gaze rested for a moment on a bright white cirque, its snow pack cold against the blue granite of the mountain. He felt it again. The pain that seared his mind and filled his gut.

"Marichu, my Mary, please get well," he repeated to himself again, as he had for days now.

He wrenched his mind back to the ranch.

"Pete, you have the lamb ready?" he said, still looking at the sky and hills. "Rosita wants it for Sunday. Big party for the boss." He turned. "Go now. You can take it tomorrow on the regular run."

Pete pulled on the brim of his battered Stetson, and threw Jose a quick look before heading for the door. "I gonna take some of those hens she likes too, and a few extra eggs."

Jose watched him leave, and then turned his attention to the kitchen, where he heard the familiar sounds of Dominga, cutting vegetables and stoking up the wood fire for lunch. They had both risen at 5:00 a.m. to start the wood stoves and begin the preparation for breakfast; steak and eggs. There were not as many men to cook for this time of year, but there were three herders and one ranch hand staying in the bunk-house and, of course, the family.

"I'm goin' to make lamb stew for the lunch, Aita," she said, now mixing pancake batter. "Maybe Marichu will drink some broth, but I don' know," she shook her head slowly. "Her fever is still strong and she is coughing. I'm goin' to make another mustard plaster *en tiempo*" She finished mixing the contents in the bowl and tested the cast iron skillet with a sprinkling of water. Steam fizzed the air.

Jose and Dominga Ancho had been at the Martin ranch for six years. The Martin was the largest ranch in a group of five that spread out across thousands of acres of irrigated land in northeastern Nevada. It supplied all the meat and produce for the Jenkins Sheep and Cattle Company, a titan Nevada ranching outfit. Each week, beef, lamb, chicken, eggs and produce were delivered to the other four ranches from the Martin to feed the ranch employees. Jose and his wife, Dominga, and their four children, lived in the small ranch house on the property.

Jose was a Navarrese, and unlike your typical Basque, he was tall and slender, not big-boned. He had dark hair and a startling handsomeness. Jose had emigrated from Spain at nineteen years old to herd sheep in the Nevada desert and had done well. He was known for his exquisite skill with horses and had worked his way up from sheepherder to a job as foreman of one of the largest spreads in the area in a matter of a few years. Dominga had also emigrated to the States at nineteen and had gone to work for cousins in Jack Creek as a cook and housekeeper at a Basque hotel. Her time there had not been pleasant and there were many nights she cried bitter tears about leaving her home in the Pyrenees. But now she was at the Martin, and she loved the small house, and took care of it as if she had put down the money herself for its purchase.

Pete Mariani, an Italian from Sicily, was the ranch gardener, and gifted in the art of making things grow. In the summer, he planted tomatoes, lettuce and zucchini by the phases of the moon, and he had come by the house that morning to tell Jose that he was wrong to kill the owls. "When you kill an owl, bad things will happen, my friend. You need to stop," he had told him. "The owls, they have a certain strength, a power."

Though he was tired, Jose's words came out like the law that they were.

"One has nothing to do with the other, my friend. *Bastante.*" Jose thought about these words now. It was unlike him to talk this way, but Pete would not stop about the owls. He wouldn't let it go.

"There is nothing good about those owls," Jose told himself. "They take what is not theirs to take."

His words were tight with his worry for Mary, with the pain of an all-night vigil outside his nine-year-old daughter's room. His voice betrayed his exhaustion. He put his hand against the doorframe of the kitchen entryway, to steady himself before talking to his wife, and then stared dumbly in at what he saw. Dominga was not standing at the sink, cutting potatoes and carrots for the stew she had talked about that morning, but rather she was sitting uncharacteristically slumped at the kitchen table, staring out the kitchen window toward the road leading into the ranch yard.

"What are you doing, Ama?" Jose asked in a low voice. He moved over to her and put a hand on her shoulder.

Dominga looked up, her eyes glazed and swollen. She held a knotted white lace handkerchief in her right hand, soaked with tears, and gripped it fiercely.

"I called the Father. He is coming."

Jose's tanned face turned pale.

"There's nothing else we can do then," he said, his voice sounding hard. "We'll wait for Father Mendiko."

Mary listened to their conversation through the thin wood of her bedroom door. "What was Pete saying about the owls?" she thought. Had she dreamed it? She heard it all, except for the last part about the priest. A cold wind rattled the splintered wood window frames in her small room, but she was burning up with fever, drifting in and out of consciousness. Her mother was just in her room, pressing something cold to her forehead. Or was she? She couldn't remember.

Mary was never sick. She and her brothers and sister attended school in a one-room schoolhouse at the "Betty O'Neil," a gold mine near the ranch. The mine owners had built it for the miners' children, but the two ranches in the immediate area also sent their children there. Mary had never missed a day of school, even in the worst of winters. But Dominga had known something was wrong when Mary came to breakfast with her hair dull and her brown eyes red and watery. Her chest hurt.

"But I want to go to school today, Ama," Mary had told Dominga. "We're learning fractions. Please?" pleaded Mary.

And so Dominga said yes, and four hours later Mary was delivered back to the ranch by a miner who had been drafted to return a sick child home. That was five days ago.

When the priest arrived at the ranch, Dominga met him at the door and led him quickly into her daughter's room. She stood behind him, crying softly, holding her string of black beads tightly in her fingers, moving from one to the next, repeating over and over again the liturgy of the rosary. "Holy Mary, Mother of God, pray for us sinners, now and at the hour of our death. Amen."

But Jose was having different thoughts. He stayed in the kitchen, sitting in the chair his wife had been in, holding his head in his hands. He looked up slowly, and vaguely noticed the green of the cottonwoods that lined the irrigation ditch close to the ranch house. He couldn't bear any more sorrow about his little girl. He was thinking about the owls.

"A wire roof would stop them from coming down into the hen yard. I should have done it long ago. I have the wire and boards behind the barn. *Bai,* that will work."

In Mary's room, Father Mendiko sat reading aloud from a small black book.

"Espiritu Sancti. Amen." The last rites. A weak voice rose from the bed.

"Please... stop," cried Mary. Her voice shook with the effort of the words and her small face convulsed in protest. "I'm not going to die!" Father Mendiko stopped reading and looked down at the little white face on the pillow. He saw a sudden terror in the brown eyes, and then an amazing strength and anger appeared that he had not seen before. "Perhaps it's not your time yet, little one," he said and knelt beside the bed, crossing himself and taking her small hand in his.

Sixty years later — Reno, Nevada

It was the shape of its head that first entered Kate's consciousness. She saw it out of the corner of her eye while she was standing at the kitchen window making dinner. It was perched on the telephone wires above the garden, near the back fence, and she could just make out the large ear-like tufts, the muscular shape of the body, and imagine the large yellow eyes, watching, above the curved black beak. It was a great horned owl.

Lying in bed now, she swallowed carefully. "Why does it have to be tonight?" she thought. A soft hooting had awakened her only a few minutes before, and she had turned on the lamp next to her bed to check out the familiar landmarks of dresser, closet and bookshelf; all there. She snuggled back into the covers, and drew her knees in close, pressing them up against the hard smoothness of her round belly, thinking about the Caesarian scheduled in a few hours. Seeing an owl tonight, especially on this night, was unnerving. Owls held a special meaning in her life. A kinship existed there, or maybe a mystical relationship, she was never sure. At the very least, she ascribed something to them out of the ordinary.

A great horned owl once landed in a weeping willow tree in the small urban backyard where Kate grew up. Her mother went in for dental surgery the day after the owl arrived and she lay in bed after that, suffering from a massive infection from the extensive dental procedure.

"He reminds me of the owls on the ranch when I was growing up," Kate's mother said, leaning back against the propped pillows on her bed. "They roosted in those old cottonwoods behind the ranch house, and we'd listen to them, night after night, hooting and calling and flying out after dark to look for food." She laughed. "Like as not, it would be my dad's chickens!"

Her reminiscing continued in a lighter voice. "We'd see them sometimes near the barn at twilight. That barn held great bags of wool, half as long as our house and about five feet high, stacked sometimes four or five bags deep. One year the price of wool was not so good and so my father decided to store the wool in the barn and see if he could do better in the spring. My brothers and sister and I spent hours and hours in and around the wool bags that winter, making forts and crawling through the tunnels. We'd hide and someone would have to find us, or we'd play follow-the-leader, sometimes diving down deep holes and then popping back up again. I would have dreams sometimes after those sweaty, scratchy days in the barn. Terrible nightmares about long, dark tunnels, and something chasing me, and in my dreams I'd see the owls fly past the open barn doors."

"One day, I remember I found a dead rabbit in the sagebrush. I got one of my brothers to put it next to the barn door and we tried to wait up all night to see an owl swoop down and get it. Of course, we fell asleep, but in the morning, it was gone."

Kate sat listening to her mother on the big bed, and they both watched the owl through the bedroom window, so exotic-looking, sitting so still on the tree branch; Kate wondered what it knew.

A soft hooting brought her back to the present and Kate wondered what the appearance of an owl tonight meant, if anything. "This is silly," she told herself, but it didn't stop the fear in her stomach. She struggled to roll over on her side, attempting to maneuver her huge belly around so that she could sit up. She thought about the Caesarean scheduled for 6:00 a.m. to deliver the baby inside her. "I just need to make it a few more hours," she told herself, and reached for her robe.

The back of her blue hospital gown was wet. She could feel something dripping onto the back of her legs. She tugged on the sleeve of the nurse standing next to her, prepping her for surgery.

"I'm wet," Kate said, squirming on the metal gurney, lifting her knees. The nurse quickly checked and then laughed as she wheeled her into the delivery room. "Your water has broken," she said. "Time to deliver a baby!"

Five pairs of eyes focused directly on her face now. She was lying in the fetal position on the draped metal table. The delivery room was filled with a hushed silence. "Give her another epidural," came the staccato words of her doctor. Another needle was stabbed into the base of her spine. Again a short wait. Nothing. The drugs, for some reason, were not having their full effect, and she could still feel the scrape of the cold metal instrument across the soles of her feet.

She closed her eyes against the intensity of the surgical lights. "Please, God, don't let anything bad happen to my baby," she prayed loudly in her mind. The fear she felt the night before, listening to the owl, was strong in her mouth. "No," she thought, gritting her teeth. "I won't let it."

Her doctor was agitated, his eyes wide behind his horn rimmed glasses. "We have to take this baby. She's starting to stress. We'll pump you with drugs as soon as she's out, but we've got to do it *now?*

Crying came next, and it was impossible to tell whose tears were whose. A little girl emerged, mouth open wide, crying, then choking on amniotic fluid. Kate heard herself ask, from what seemed very far away, "Is she all right, what's happening?"

One of the nurses wrapped the baby in a blanket and held her face down next to Kate's, but Kate was starting to lose consciousness from the arsenal of painkillers being pumped into her system. "Don't worry, she's doing well," the doctor said, leaning over her again and reaching for the sutures.

"Doing well," Kate thought, mouthing the words, as she lapsed into unconsciousness in a thick fog of drugs.

Kate struggled to see through the thick canopy of the branches. She knew they were in there, somewhere. She found herself in a lush green world interspersed with sparkling shafts of sunlight. A strong breeze gusted, rustling the leaves, and the top boughs of the tree swayed slowly back and forth in the wind, like waves. Focusing now, she could see four of them; a female perched on a branch, holding a large mouse in her beak, its long tail swinging limply, back and forth, with every turn of her great head. Three gray, downy owlets peered up at her out of a large stick nest, yellow eyes blinking. The female quickly dropped the mouse into the nest and proceeded to rip its body apart with her strong beak and talons. She dropped the pieces into the owlets' open mouths, bit by bit, and they ate voraciously. The tiny owlets then climbed slowly out of the nest, their round bodies awkwardly maneuvering onto the thick branch, and they started forward, step by slow step. Suddenly, an enormous gust of wind roared through the branches, making a thundering noise. Kate watched in horror as the small bodies rocked back and forth, struggling to maintain their balance. The tiny talons clung fiercely to the wood, down and feathers flying in all directions, and then, just as suddenly as it had appeared, the gust passed and it was still.

Nine years later — Nevada desert

"Mommy, look at the bluebirds!" the small girl yelled, running across the campground, pointing at the birds flying overhead. She stopped suddenly, lifting her hand to shield her eyes from the late afternoon sun.

"No, those are piñon jays," said Mary, packing up the rest of the dinner and putting it into a cardboard box sitting next to her on the picnic table. "Listen to the sound they make.

You can see them in the fall all flying together in big flocks."

Kate and her family had spent the day in Louis Canyon, a childhood haunt of her mother's, hiking and exploring an area that had changed little in the past fifty years. It was about five miles away from where her mother was born, and Mary had reminisced fondly during dinner about growing up on the Nevada desert. They played a game called Scrambled Legs, where the top half of an animal appeared on one card, and the corresponding bottom half appeared on another. Cards were drawn, sometimes matching the head of a walrus with the legs of a tortoise, or the bottom of a dog with the top of a giraffe, until someone got a match and won the game. When Kate's daughter drew the head of an owl, she said, "Mommy, this is my favorite animal!" Kate was surprised. She didn't remember ever talking to her about owls before.

"My dad used to kill the owls that were on the ranch," said Mary matter-of-factly. The girl's eyes grew round in disbelief.

"Why, Muggie, why did he kill them?" The little girl wanted to know. "Did he eat them?"

"I saw a great horned owl on our back fence the night before you were born." Kate told her. This led to more excitement and questions as they walked back to the truck and packed up to leave. It was a dark night, no moon, and the highway stretched ahead only as far as the reach of the truck headlights. Kate sat in the passenger seat, and turned her head to look back at her mother and her daughter, sound asleep in the back seat. A female voice crooned softly on the truck radio. Suddenly, something out of the corner of Kate's eye pulled her head back around to see a large pair of wings appear in the frame of the front windshield, and then just as suddenly, disappear again, into the dark.

Mary opened her eyes for a second and then leaned her head back against the seat cushion.

"Mommy?" came a voice from the back seat. "What was that?"

Kate looked back again at her child, head resting again in her grandmother's lap, eyes open wide. "Shhh, it's just an owl," she said. "Go back to sleep."

Basking in a Different Sun: The Story of Conchi Mendiolea

Bianka Vidonja Balanzategui

Introduction

On a steamy, tropical day in North Queensland in northeastern Australia the rain falls so heavily that it fills the backyard swimming pool to overflowing. Inside the air-conditioned house, an old woman lies oblivious to the drumming rains of summer, her mind lost to Alzheimer's disease. Conchi Mendiolea ministers tenderly to her, sponging her, changing her diaper and nightdress, applying cologne and kissing her tenderly on the brow as she settles her back into bed. Afterwards, Conchi's husband, John Mendiolea, feeds her soup, and when he moves too slowly, she says to him, in what little language she is now capable of, *"ala, pues"* (hurry up). She is Amoma, the grandmother, Conchi's mother, and the life of the house. The activities of its occupants and visitors revolve around her. Her bed, set up with all the necessities to make her life as comfortable as possible, stands just inside the front door in a large tiled room. The eight years that Conchi and Johnny have spent caring for the bedridden woman have exacted a great personal cost, but they continue to look after her at home because of both family custom and their own deep personal attachment to her.

Behind the bed an unfinished painting hangs on the wall. Its subject is unmistakable. It is Conchi, holding her dead mother in her arms. In the picture, as in life, Conchi is kiss-

ing her mother's brow, but not until the inevitable happens
and Amoma passes will the painting be finished. Meanwhile
Amoma is 95 years old and in good physical health, despite
her debilitating mental condition, and so life must go on.

On a table underneath that painting stands another canvas, also unfinished, of a *torero* (bullfighter), inspired by a recent brief trip home to Spain. The acrylic colors are bright and
lively. "Spanish colors," Conchi calls them, "nice and bright
and pure." [1] The walls of this suburban home in Townsville
(Queensland) are lined with similar paintings. They are all
the work of this vibrant woman, and inspired by her Basque
heritage, her past and present life, her Australian experiences,
her love of family, her relationship with her mother and her
religious sentiment.

Conchi Mendiolea, the Woman

At the turn of the twentieth century the Herbert River district
of northern Queensland in Australia began to experience a
substantial immigration of southern European people, principally from Spain and Italy. The first immigrants came to
cut sugar cane for the 1907 harvest season and were brought
to Australia under a contract labor scheme devised by the
Colonial Sugar Refining Company. Most of those first immigrants left when their contract ended, but a few remained
and bought farms. [2] The first Basque is believed to have arrived in Queensland in 1882, [3] and the first to arrive in the

1   Conchi Mendiolea, personal communication, September 30, 1993,
handwritten notes.

2   William A. Douglass, *From Italy to Ingham* (Queensland: University of
Queensland Press, 1995), p. 104.

3   Large-scale Basque migration to Australia really took off in the
1930s. "There, almost to the man, they became involved in the sugar
industry as cane cutters. The job is well paid but requires considerable
immigrant labor, since it is so extremely dirty and tedious that few Australians are willing to do it. Over the years the Basques of northeastern

Herbert River district was Aniceto Menchaca, who came to
Sydney in 1907 from Bilbao. It took him four months to complete the move to the Herbert River district where he would
eventually supply cane to the Victoria Sugar Mill. In 1911 he
brought out his brother Juan, and soon others followed, including members of the Balanzategui, Badiola, Elortegui and
Mendiolea families.[4] There thus started a pattern of ethnic
migration from the Basque Country that would have important social consequences for this corner of Australia.

Johnny Mendiolea's parents, Tomas and Teresa, migrated
to Australia from their hometown of Aulestia (Bizkaia) in
1924. They immediately moved to Ingham in Queensland
where a number of men from Aulestia had previously settled
and found work in the sugar industry. The Mendioleas arrived with their two children and Teresa was already pregnant
with a third, who would be the first of their offspring born in
the Herbert River district. The Mendioleas also paid for the
passages of three other men from Aulestia, who traveled with
them to Australia, thus beginning the family practice of sponsoring and helping other migrants, a role that Johnny and
Conchi would inherit in their turn.

Shortly after their arrival, Tomas found work as a farm
hand, and later as a canecutter, while Teresa worked as a
cook for an Italian canecutting gang. In 1927 they acquired
a boarding house in Ingham. Tomas, however, continued to
cut cane while Teresa concentrated on running the boarding
house and looking after the guests. Three years later they sold
the boarding house and leased a cane farm at Long Pocket,
some distance from Ingham town. In 1933 they moved to a

Australia established an ethnic group reputation as the best cane-cutters,
and several rose through the ranks to acquire their own sugar holdings."
William A. Douglass and Jon Bilbao, *Amerikanuak: Basques in the New
World* (Reno: University of Nevada Press, 1975), pp. 411-12.

4   Conchi Mendiolea, personal communication, September 30, 1993,
handwritten notes.

farm that was a bit closer to town, and then in January 1945, they bought the Zavatarro farm, located only four kilometers from Ingham. By this time, they had five children: Rufino and Antonio (born in Spain), together with Aniceto, Juan and Dolores (born in Australia). In 1948 Tomas and Teresa returned to Spain for a holiday and while there, they invited some nephews to come to Australia and "try their luck," once again playing the role of facilitators for young migrants.

Fifteen years later, in 1962, their son Juan (or Johnny) also went to the Basque Country for a lengthy holiday and there he met his future bride. Conchi Mendiolea was born María Concepción Arrasate to Fermina Cajigas and Julio Arrasate on November 30, 1944 in Lekeitio in the province of Bizkaia in the Basque Country of Spain. She was only seventeen when she met Australian-born Johnny, during his first visit to Euskal Herria (the Basque Country). He didn't go specifically to look for a Basque wife, but one year into his stay, Conchi caught his eye. The following year, when Conchi was just eighteen years old, they were married. She returned to Australia with him "with a lot of hope but with a little fear in my heart,"[5] to live in the family home on the farm his parents bought, the old Zavatarro place, situated between the village of Trebonne and the town of Ingham in the Herbert River Valley of North Queensland. Thus in 1963 Johnny brought Conchi home to a large and imposing cement house. "It was a huge house," recalls Conchi, "not only in size but in manner, so that all the Basques and many Spanish migrants in need of help came there, and they were welcomed with open arms."[6]

Johnny's father, Tomas, had died in April of 1950, so when the newlyweds first arrived in Australia, they lived with his mother, Teresa. When Teresa died, Conchi and Johnny

---

5   Ibid.

6   Ibid.

took over her role in the community. "We acquired most of the work of looking after the migrants' needs," remembers Conchi, "as well as those of my children and my parents, and many other things that came my way." [7] Over time, Conchi and Johnny had four sons of their own: John, Tomas, Michael, and Stephen. Then in 1967 they brought Conchi's parents to Australia to live with them. However, Julio, Conchi's father, as a sailor used to lengthy periods away from home throughout his life, could not cope with the domesticated lifestyle of his daughter's family and returned, alone, to the Basque Country where he died in 1988. By contrast, Fermina, Conchi's mother, remained in North Queensland.

Spanish migration to North Queensland peaked in the 1950s. Some of the migration was self-initiated, when people decided to try their luck in Australia. In other cases the migration was sponsored, either by the Australian government or by the Queensland Cane Growers. Most of the migrants were single males employed in seasonal work such as canecutting and construction. By the late 1960s about one hundred of them remained in the Herbert River district, of whom eighty-five were Basque. These Basques included several familes, such as the Jayos, Unamunos, Longartes and Laucericas. [8] The Jayo family followed the example of earlier migrants and settled in the small village of Trebonne, where Basques congregated on the weekends to meet socially and maintain old world traditions. For example, they played *pelota* in the town's *fronton* and stones were brought from the Basque Country for stonelifting contests. The partyers would also lay a wooden floor over the grass so that they could dance, and others played *mus,* a Basque card game.

The Herbert River district Basques also liked to gather in the Zavatarro house on the Mendiolea farm. There, solitary

7   Ibid.

8   Ibid.

migrants found the hospitality and companionship that they had left behind in the Basque Country. "But there was more," adds Conchi. "They also found compassion and the feeling that somebody cared about them." [9] Those who went to the house looking for help would inevitably be invited to stay for a few days until they could find work and a more permanent place to live. Others who lived in hotels would show up at the house whenever they felt lonely, for a weekend at the Mendiolea place was a good way to experience a taste of home and a bit of family life. Johnny often helped them apply for naturalization or for their pension, and he translated for them when they had to deal with lawyers and government officials. As the migrants aged, Conchi found herself visiting the sick in the hospital, identifying the bodies of those who passed away, organizing funerals and burials, and writing to the families in Spain with the sad news of a loved one's death.

The cadence of life on a sugar cane farm is determined by the rhythms of the canecutting season, punctuated by slack time, and followed by the time for planting. In the days of manual cutting, gangs of cutters harvested the cane. Many were itinerant workers who descended on the sugar towns in June for the harvest season and left in December at the beginning of the slack season. Thereafter they sought construction jobs in the cities, or looked for work in other crop-growing areas of Queensland, such as Mareeba on the northern Table-lands, where tobacco was cultivated and required much itinerant labor for harvesting and grading.

Even though harvesting today is done with machines and the seasonal migration of laborers is no longer necessary, there is still a lively sense of urgency and activity during the cutting season and a corresponding down time during the slack. Conchi's daily activities were determined by the work that was in progress on the farm. Some chores, however, were

---

9   Ibid.

never-ending. She cooked, did the washing and labored to keep the large house clean, but it was a struggle, with verandas all around that caught the black ash from the cane fires and gave meager protection to the rooms inside when the torrential rains of the wet season were driven by the wind from all angles.

When Johnny's parents died, the farm was divided four ways among the brothers, but fate dealt Johnny a cruel blow when two of his siblings died at a comparatively early age. Another tragedy ocurred when a nephew, just a toddler, died in a farm accident. Then Johnny's health began to fail. According to Conchi, "it was a worry, because I had four small children. You know what happens when the father is sick. Many times we thought he was dying. And it affected me a lot personally. I used to think, what can I do on a farm with all these kids, and how can I go on with life, not speaking proper English here in this country? Yes, I had good friends who were ready to help, but you have to live your own life. So it worried me a lot, and caused a lot of problems in my mind." [10] Nevertheless, Conchi prided herself on her independence. She felt that everyone had their own problems, and remained determined not to burden anyone else with hers. In addition, she wanted to be open to other women and ready for them if they came to her with their problems. Clearly, then, she preferred helping others to asking for help for herself.

During her early years in Australia, Conchi battled terrible loneliness, brought on by her lack of fluency in English. Being Australian-born, Johnny spoke fluent English, but that just made Conchi more self-conscious about her lack of ability in the language. It was especially hard when she had to go to the doctor, or when everyone around them at social events was speaking English. Later it was also problematic for her when the children went to school. However, she was deter-

---

10   Ibid.

mined to overcome what she saw as a terrible problem so she began to take English lessons by correspondence, and persevered until she could read and write capably. Once she conquered the language, her loneliness eased and she felt much happier. She also felt more qualified to help other migrants. Thereafter, although she would always speak with a strong accent and occasionally awkward syntax, this did not prevent her from attending university lectures and completing written homework assignments later in life.

The birth of her children brought Conchi great happiness. "When they were born," she admits, "I realized that I was married, and I had to live up here. I had to go on with life and look after my children, even though I was born a migrant." [11] This realization was a turning point and it enabled her to move on and accept her situation. She vowed to make the best of her life in North Queensland but there remained many problems. "When I was twenty-six," she recalls, "I started with nervous problems. It was pre-natal and postnatal depression, but nobody knew then what it was. So I coped with that terrible problem by myself, all those years." [12]

Conchi knew how to drive a car, so she was not physically restricted to the farm, but she had little or no time to drive around and socialize: "I never used to go to anyone's place because I had too much to do at home, with four children and my parents, and later my uncle and aunt were there, too." [13] At that time her parents lived nearby and led independent lives, but her mother had poor eyesight that gradually degenerated into blindness, and Conchi tried to help as much as she could. Her paternal aunt and uncle also lived in Ingham, and Conchi would often bring them out to the farm on the weekends to visit.

---

11   Ibid.

12   Ibid.

13   Ibid.

Even though she conquered her loneliness and coped with the work of a farm wife, Conchi was aware of yearnings that she could not fulfill. In the Basque Country, for example, she had been a dressmaker. After coming to Australia, she initially sewed as a favor for relatives and friends, then later to earn money. She eventually earned enough this way to buy an apartment in her home town of Lekeitio. However, sewing was never enough to satisfy her creative urges. As she recalls, "I always wanted to learn to paint, but I kept it to myself because I had no opportunity to develop my talent. Instead, I turned my energy to fixing up my house. I was always painting the walls and hanging wallpaper, fixing this and that, making things beautiful in the Spanish or Basque way. So I think that desire to express myself artistically was inside of me since I was young." [14]

But Conchi's life was headed inexorably toward the world of art. In 1990 a decision was made to sell the family farm. By then, Johnny and Dolores were the only Mendiolea siblings still living. Johnny, Conchi, Stephen, and Amoma stayed on at the Zavatarro house until 1994, when they moved to Townsville. The house was then rented out until they sold it several years later. Conchi recalls that, "when I came up to Townsville, I got sick and had nervous problems, and then came the change of life. I had a breakdown because of those problems. I was tired of looking after Amoma." [15]

Conchi felt that the move to Townsville was for the best, although she realized that it was a painful displacement for Johnny. When the last of the old gentlemen they looked after died, they felt free to leave the district. Moreover, as Conchi was growing older and feeling her years, a smaller house to take care of sounded appealing. In addition, there were other factors that justified the move, including better job possibili-

14 Ibid.

15 Ibid.

ties and educational opportunities for Stephen. Furthermore, if Johnny fell ill again, there were hospitals nearby and support systems in place to help care for Amoma, and as for herself, there was a university available where she could pursue her studies.

"When I came to Townsville," Conchi remembers, "I needed to get out of the house and do something. The only thing that appealed to me was to study art. I was thinking, this will be very hard for me because I have no language, not enough English. But I decided to give it a go, so I went to college. And I did very well. I don't know why, but I passed everything."[16] Conchi enrolled in TAFE (Technical and Further Education) to pursue her artistic impulse. She had already started painting before enrolling, but most of her works were completed as part of her art course there, which she undertook at first for therapeutic value and then for the opportunity to learn to paint properly. However, what started as a hobby subsequently blossomed into a life's ambition: "I wanted to be an artist. All my life, I wanted to work with color. Someday, maybe, I would like to teach painting and drawing."[17]

The TAFE Diploma course equipped Conchi with the credentials she needed to enroll at James Cook University in Townsville, where she pursued a Bachelor's degree in visual arts. Even though she was pursuing her dream, however, the physical toll of menopause, her husband's illness, and the sleepless nights spent looking after her mother, kept her from doing as well at school as she wanted to. All of these factors combined to worsen her chronic depression, and finally she decided to seek professional help. That decision made all the difference. Even though the pressures continued, Conchi felt she was able to cope, and she became more confident in her studies, and even mastered the language of art.

---

16   Ibid.

17   Ibid.

Conchi Mendiolea, the Artist

Conchi paints mostly in an abstract style that she describes as coming naturally to her. The subject of many of her paintings is her native land, the Basque Country. Using acrylic on canvas, textured with cement and glue, she captures the contours of the mountains where she was born and raised. "When I think about my youth," she recalls, "growing up, I think about those beautiful green colors, and the beautiful people there, and the sea, the lovely sea. I remember how happy I was there. My parents and family looked after me and loved me. I was very lucky. I had a wonderful family who cared for me very much." [18]

But there were darker memories, too, for she was born in the immediate aftermath of the Spanish Civil War (1936-39), into a Basque society that was suffering the severe consequences of postwar economic hardship and the dictatorial repression of the Franco regime. [19] She spoke sadly of the loss of her uncle and aunt in the bombing of Gernika in 1937, and of how her parents lost a two-and-a-half-year-old daughter to pneumonia during the war. These feelings affect Conchi's art. She selects her colors "to give meanings to feelings" and describes her paintings as possessing "all my Spanish colors, nice and bright and pure." [20]

Yet several paintings are singular for their lack of vibrancy. These represent the canefields and countryside of the Herbert River district. They stand in marked contrast to her works depicting the Basque Country. They are dark and somber. One of them depicts a child at play, the little girl that Conchi never

---

18   Ibid.

19   See, for example, Manuel Gonzalez Portilla and José María Garmendia, *La posguerra en el País Vasco. Política, acumulación, miseria* (Donostia: Kriselu, 1988).

20   Conchi Mendiolea, personal communication, September 30, 1993, handwritten notes.

had. She reconciles her regret over never having a daughter by painting images of female children. Another painting depicts the Zavatarro house. She painted it in tones of red, a color that carries ambivalent connotations in her paintings, used to depict both love and hate, and even Basque sentimentality. The images of the Zavatarro house are rather disturbing. In contrast, a painting of Cassady Beach, near Ingham, where the family's beach house was located, reveals much light and happiness.

Conchi and her family spent many happy weeks there every slack season when the children were young. For example, they often spent Christmas day there with over forty people, family and friends, sitting down to dinner. In the painting the beach is peaceful with small boats moored on the sand. It captures the joy and delight that Conchi found in the Australian summer sunshine and clear blue days at the beach.

Another part of her work expresses Conchi's interest in history. Although a lot of Spanish and Basque people migrated to Australia, for many it was not their first choice of destination. As such, these people experienced secondary migration, where individuals migrate several times in their life, including return migration (temporary or permanent) to their homelands. [21] Some migrants, such as Johnny's father, settled first in the Americas, then returned home and only migrated to Australia later. Johnny's grandfather, Braulio Mendiolea, also migrated to the western United States in the early 1900s where he worked, among other jobs, as a sheepherder and miner. Tomas, Johnny's father, left the Basque Country in 1908 to join him but upon his arrival, he found that Braulio had disappeared under mysterious circumstances. Tomas

---

21 See William A. Douglass, "Factors in the Formation of the New-World Basque Emigrant Diaspora," in William A. Douglass, ed. *Essays in Basque Social Anthropology and History* (Reno: Basque Studies Program, 1989), p. 260.

worked in the United States as a sheep-herder and after several years moved on to Argentina where he worked with cattle in the Pampas, returning to the Basque Country in 1919.

Similarly, some members of Conchi's father's family, the Arrasate branch, migrated to Chile and Argentina and their descendents still live in Buenos Aires. [22] During her studies, Conchi researched the migration of Basque men to the western United States from 1849 onwards. In the U.S., she discovered, they worked as shepherds and led lonely, hard, and dangerous lives. They left records of their yearnings, concerns and interests in the form of tree carvings on the trunks of aspens. They carved names, dates, and images on the trees, pertaining to a variety of subjects including religion, politics, art, and sexual fantasies. This research served as Conchi's inspiration for a painting in which she attempted to express the history of the Basque people in the United States.

Yet another painting was inspired by the Spanish Inquisition. In the work Conchi expresses anger and sorrow for the people who lost their lives. The color purple, representing the Church, predominates and feelings are expressed as abstract images through a surface relief technique. Other paintings are less abstract. One concerning a Spanish girl playing a guitar and another portraying several people picking fruit in the summertime are imbued with warmth and activity. One of her trips home inspired her to paint a Basque man in national costume, holding an *ikurriña* (the Basque flag). In this painting, a special favorite of the family, she externalizes her feel-

---

22   The Basque emigration experience is remarkable for the variety of destinations it encompasses and, by definition, the historical legacy this has left for individual families. In one study of a small Basque village, carried out in the mid 1960s (close to the time that Conchi moved to Australia), it was revealed that 179 males (out of a total of 429) had emigrated at some time (either returning or staying in the country of their chosen destination). Of these, 107 had been to the American West, 41 had gone to Australia, 12 to Argentina, 10 to Uruguay and the remaining 9 to Mexico, Peru, Cuba, Chile and Africa. See Douglass and Bilbao, *Amerikanuak,* pp. 5-6.

ings about the country she left in 1963 and the changes that have taken place since.

Another category of paintings are those created to serve a cathartic purpose. These paintings are mostly autobiographical, dealing with her life as a child in the Basque Country and her later years on the farm in Australia. In one such work, she depicts the Spanish feast of San Juan, celebrated every July in Donostia-San Sebastián, the capital city of Gipuzkoa. "I was seven years old," remembers Conchi. "I remember at night they built big fires. I was thinking about that when I started this painting. Everybody was happy and singing. I was little, and two men took me by the hands, and they jumped over the fire, but they went too low, and I got burnt. It was terribly painful. I'll never forget that day. I got such a fright. So I did this painting to take the fear out of that memory. This is how I work." [23]

Marrying into Johnny's large family meant forming both new family relationships and good working partnerships as the farm was a business enterprise. Life was not easy, and Conchi struggled over the years to muster the emotional and physical energy needed to maintain those relationships. "I paint to forget all the things that happened over there," she recalls, "I want to cover all the problems, too. But with the problems go good and bad things, and in order to forget the bad things, I am covering up the good things, too. All the beautiful times we had there. Johnny and I, we had a good marriage, because we got on together very good." [24]

Conchi's family was the central focus of her life and the source of her daily joy, but she also wrestled with the responsibilities of caring for others and the restrictions placed upon a woman by her family situation. All these experiences found

23 Conchi Mendiolea, personal communication, September 30, 1993, handwritten notes.

24 Ibid.

expression in her paintings. In one work, the all-seeing eye of a possessive European man stares down from one side of the canvas, his wife and children on the other side, always within his view. The woman is bound to the house and family through the purple of the patriarchal Church, as its rites, traditions and laws reinforce the subordination of women to men and family. This is a painting that Conchi would never sell because it portrays an essential aspect of her culture, the way she perceived that women were treated in Europe. While in her opinion this is not an accurate reflection of her marriage to Johnny, she does believe that it represents the relationship between her own mother and her father.

Conchi's father was a sailor. He was used to living away from his family for months at a time, and when on shore, he could not cope with all the associated problems of domestic life. Toward the end of his life, he just wanted to live in peace, by himself. He thus left Australia to return to the Basque Country, and he left his wife in Conchi's care. Conchi was dismayed and upset by his abandonment of her mother, but at the same time she loved her father. "He didn't have much education," she remembers. "He was brought up alone without a mother because they lost their mother when they were young. I remember him as a good man." [25]

As such, and with children still at home to look after, Conchi was forced to assume the care of her mother who, due to increasing ill health, was rapidly becoming dependent on others. Consequently she personally experienced the role of female nurturer bound to the family and male controller who could disassociate himself from family responsibilities on a whim, and she expresses these experiences in her painting. The painting entitled "My Grandfather" was inspired by her own grandfather, by her father, and by all the men of the Basque Country. "Over there, men like to go to sea or to work,

---

25 Ibid.

then come home, and then go to the *taberna* and have a good time. This painting represents the Basque gentlemen. It represents my grandfather. He was a man who liked the *taberna* more than home."[26] Yet another painting features the image of a hand, a symbol she uses for both the process of artistic creation and the masculine force. "The hand," she argues, "represents the mind, because from the mind the thought goes to the hand, and the artist works with the hand. And it represents the power of the men, the power of Basque men over Basque women. It represents the hand of my father."[27]

By contrast, the love that Conchi felt for her mother was both a burden and an inspiration. Her responsibilities brought on physical and emotional exhaustion. At the same time, this same love spurred her on to heights of artistic creativity. The paintings inspired by the love for her mother can be brutally realistic portrayals of her eventual death, or abstract delicate portrayals incorporating her mother's *mantilla,* which she often wore to Church, and fan. The fan is cut into three pieces to represent the love of the three people who cared for her at the end of her life.Conchi's paintings make it clear that she is dreading the loss of her mother and uses the work as a vehicle to prepare herself for the day when she passes away. Her feelings are evident in a poem that she embossed for an assignment for one of her TAFE classes:

The Sun shone with all its light,
But one fine day the fog arrived,
Bringing with it a cruel sour wind.
It took with it, bit by bit, all that I loved.
My loving Mother, Mother of my Heart.
Soul and Hope, one day I will cross the
Fog and I will reach you to embrace you

---

26   Ibid.

27   Ibid.

With all my Soul. That day the sun will
shine again in my Heart, which was filled
with Sadness.
Your loving daughter Conchi
R.I.P.

Although she dreads the loss of her mother, Conchi does
not fear death itself. Once, in Ingham, she was called to the
mortuary to identify the body of a fellow Basque. When she
arrived, she was informed that yet another Basque man of her
acquaintance lay dead in the compartment above the first fellow. In that room, at that moment, she lost all fear of death.

She signs all her work with her first name, Conchi. "This
is my work," she states proudly, "Conchi makes this work, not
Mendiolea. This is me. It has nothing to do with the others.
When I am painting, I am thinking only about my work. I
don't think about anything else. Painting is an important
part of my life and who I am. I think it's very important to
be yourself." [28] After working in different mediums, Conchi
found that she preferred painting to drawing, and sculpting
to working in ceramics. As she herself says, "I feel more free
working with bigger pieces, with sculpture and painting. My
feelings come easier. I prefer the bigger canvasses." [29] Her
use of colors is dictated by what she wishes to express:

I use blue for the heavens, white for spirituality,
black for death. But purple can be death, too, or it
can represent the Chruch. And you can see that I use
a lot of purple because my mother was very sick for
a long time. We were expecting her death from day
to day. I was always expecting that something would
happen. With Johnny, too, when he had a heart
attack, he was very close to dying. Those feelings

28   Ibid.

29   Ibid.

would come out in my paintings as the color purple, purple, purple. I use red for several things. Happiness, anxiety, or an excess of emotion. I use red when I'm happy. I'm usually happy with my children, so I use red to express that, but if I'm a little upset with them, I'll paint a little blue or yellow in the mix. All of an artist's emotions can be expressed through color. [30]

In July 1998 Conchi was invited to exhibit her work in the local focus space of the Perc Tucker Gallery in Townsville. The exhibit, which was very well received, was entitled "Dreamings from the Basque Country" and included paintings, sculptures, and ceramics. The sense of Basqueness that inspired Conchi's works in the exhibit was not derived from nostalgia for her physically distant cultural heritage, but rather from an everyday Basque reality in Australia. Both Basque and Spanish are still spoken in Conchi's home. All of Conchi's sons speak Spanish, and John and Tomas can also speak Basque. Reminders of the country of her birth abound in the house in Townsville. [31] Conchi often thinks about her identity: "We carry on with our food and our way of life, and of course that means with the way I was brought up. We took some ways from the Australian people and some from the Italians in Ingham, too. After so many years here, you always end up borrowing from other cultures, but generally, I try to carry on the Basque culture in our food and in the way we live." [32]

30   Ibid.

31   This would confirm what Douglass terms the "demonstrated ethnic staying power of Basques both in their European homeland and in the Basque emigrant diasporas." See William A. Douglass, "Creating the New Basque Diaspora," in William A. Douglass, Carmelo Urza, Linda White and Joseba Zulaika, eds. *Basque Politics and Nationalism on the Eve of the Millennium* (Reno: Basque Studies Program, 1999), p. 209.

32   Conchi Mendiolea, personal communication, September 30, 1993, handwritten notes.

The Catholic church continues to be a source of spiritual sustenance for both Conchi and her husband. Johnny has resumed an active role in his community church in Townsville and as Conchi herself states, "every day, the older I get, the more I think of God. Maybe it's because I'm always at home. It gives me good feelings to think about God. It relaxes me. And it gives me the will to go on in my mind with my mother's problems and when Johnny got sick. It gives me peace and helps me accept the good and the bad that comes my way." [33]

Conchi has a photo of herself with her third son, Michael, on his wedding day. Her youthful good looks give no hint of the hard times she has endured. With the birth of Michael's first child, Adan Michael, born on Christmas day of 1998, she became a grandmother. But the gray-haired, plump and bespectacled grandmother figure of storybooks has nothing to do with Conchi, a classic raven-haired beauty with a still youthful figure, sparkling eyes and expressive mouth. She was present in Ingham when Adan was born, and captured the event on film. After the birth of her grandson, which Conchi feels was expedited by her prayers at Lourdes during a 1998 visit, she was inspired to paint a series of religious works. "These paintings will reflect my Basque heritage because our people are very Catholic," she confides. "I was brought up a strict Catholic, and I want to create paintings that express my gratitude for all the gifts that God has given us." [34]

Conchi also integrates photography into her art. She experiments with light and color, and uses the results to aid her in her painting. Conchi's goal has never been to sell her paintings, but they have begun to sell themselves. One of her works was chosen to illustrate a postcard advertising the "Fried Fire Spectacular" held in Townsville on May 11, 1998. More important, however, than selling is the peace that painting has

33 Ibid.

34 Ibid.

brought to Conchi's life. Her art not only assists in reconciling the past with the present, but it also prepares her for the future. It gives her the strength to go on, and it motivates her to keep growing every day. She sets her easel within a meter of her mother's bed, allowing her to keep a watchful eye as she works. While Amoma sleeps, Conchi paints. Her canvasses express all that she is, including her Basqueness. "This is me," says Conchi. "All that I am is in the painting." [35]

Postscript

Since this article was first written, Johnny and Conchi have moved to a smaller home in Townsville. Their generosity and hospitality to all who come to their home continues unabated. Stephen has left home, Juan has married and he and his wife Allison had their first child, Ethan, on October 9, 2000. Michael and his wife Tricia are presently expecting their second child. Tomas is still working for QANTAS as an International Air Steward. Conchi has successfully completed a Bachelor of Visual Arts and has no further study plans for the present. Meanwhile her paintings are enjoying a wider audience. When the new Townsville General Hospital opened, Conchi generously donated several of her works for display in the oncology unit.

The most significant change in their lives has been the death of Amoma, whose funeral was held in Ingham on August 14, 2002. The poem that Conchi had written several years before anticipating the "fog" and "cruel, sour wind" that would descend on her when her mother died was read in both Spanish and English at the funeral. Johnny and Conchi left for Euskal Herria on November 7, 2002 for an extended visit.

---

35   Ibid.

Emiliana de Zubeldia

Estibaliz Gastesi

The Basque pianist and composer Emiliana de Zubeldia was born in Salinas de Oro, a small town in Navarra, on 6 December 1888. She was baptized, as was the custom, on the following day. By 1890 her family had moved to Pamplona, attracted by the cultural renaissance that the provincial capital was experiencing at the time. This move was particularly beneficial to Emiliana's musical upbringing, since Pamplona sponsored a wealth of musical activities by bands, *txistularis* (players of the Basque flute), fanfares, military bands, classical music ensembles, the Orfeón Pamplonés, and, during summertime, matinee concerts with the great violinist Pablo Sarasate, a native of the city.

Emiliana's first music lessons were imparted by her older brother, Nestor. He even used to compose small pieces specifically for her. At the age of five, she gave her first public recital. Three years later, she began studying piano with Joaquín Maga at the Academia Municipal de Música de Pamplona. By the age of fifteen she had received the intermediate certificate from Madrid's Conservatorio de Música y Declamación, returning to the Spanish capital two years later, in 1906, to be examined for the advanced level. After graduating with honors, Emiliana decided to further enhance her musical studies with a sojourn in Paris.

Enrolled at the Schola Cantorum, the young Basque musician came under the tuition of Vicent D'Indy and Blanche Selva, studying in greater detail subjects such as music theory and history. It was during that time that Emiliana discovered the works of Johann Sebastian Bach, a composer that she would revere for the rest of her life. However, this period of intense study was interrupted in 1908, when, on returning home to Pamplona for the Christmas vacation, her father died suddenly. The traumatic effect of her father's death subsequently forced her to end her studies in Paris and begin a new life. It was in this abrupt way that Emiliana launched a professional career in order to help her family financially. At first she taught privately, but soon invitations to give recitals and concerts arrived from the most important theaters. In 1914, she performed at the Biarritz Casino, Bordeaux, Bayonne, and the Gran Casino of San Sebastian. In 1917, she performed in Madrid at the Círculo de Bellas Artes, the Ateneo, the Hotel Ritz, and the Salón Novedades, as well as in Pamplona — specifically in the Gayarre Theater, where she featured the works of the Basque composer Father Donostia. She also performed with the Sociedad Coral and Orfeón Pamplonés.

In 1919, she married Joaquín Fuentes Pascual, an electrician who had graduated from the Escuela Industrial de Artes y Oficios. A year later, Emiliana achieved first place in a faculty search from the Academia Municipal de Pamplona. At the same time she continued to be active as musician and composer. In 1922, she was granted sabbatical leave in order to continue her studies in Paris. Thereafter, she enjoyed her life in the French capital until 1924, when she discovered that her husband was having an extramarital affair. The shock of this discovery became the second turning point of Emiliana's life. Not wanting to confront the situation with her family, she would postpone her return to Pamplona for almost the rest of her life. First, she accepted concert engagements throughout the world, and later moved permanently to America.

Notwithstanding the personal upheavals of these years, during her second stay in Paris, Emiliana composed works such as *La muñeca de vidrio* (The Glass Doll) and the song *Guajira.* She also presented her works in a concert at the Salle Clarige. While based in France, she also returned to Madrid, where she received the diploma of Professor. In 1926 she undertook another European concert tour, which included capitals such as London, Paris, and Geneva, besides several other major cities in Italy, Belgium, and Germany. On this tour she premiered many of her own compositions, which were also being edited by the *Revue Musicale* of Paris. Thereafter, on the death of her mother in 1927, Emiliana accepted a long series of concerts through the American continent.

The trip started in Rio de Janeiro, where she formed a trio with violinist Alfonso Geper and cellist Newton Pádua. The Zubeldia-Pádua-Geper Trio soon became a prominent ensemble among Brazilian musical circles, performing many pieces by Emiliana herself. One of their most favorite works was the *Trio España* — originally written for the Trio Cabart of Paris — which consists of three movements full of colorist effects. Another interesting composition is *Berceuse de Palmeras de Brasil,* a work that highlights Emiliana's interest in different musical cultures. The tour continued in São Paulo, where, besides the chamber concerts, Emiliana gave recitals of Spanish music in many halls (such as the Instituto Nacional de Musica Espanola), always receiving favorable reviews.

In 1929, the composer went to Uruguay, where she made contact with important poets, resulting in the composition of many songs such as *El buen día convertido* (The Good Day Transformed), with lyrics by Juana de Ibarbourou. Besides the vocal works, Emiliana also wrote instrumental pieces such as the *Capricho Basko* (A Basque Capriccio) for guitar, in which elements of Basque folk music — such as the *zortziko* rhythm — were especially prominent. This growing involvement with Basque immigrant societies reached its culmination during the composer's stay in Argentina. There she performed at the Centro Laurak-Bat, the Acción Nacionalista Vasca, the Centro Vasco Francés, the Centro Navarro, the Zazpirak-Bat, the Euskaldunak Denak Bat, and the Seminario Gure Herria. That same year (1929), she participated in a grandiose Basque festival sponsored by all the immigrant centers located at the time in Argentina. The event featured not only traditional folk, but also classical music, with many pieces composed by Emiliana being choreographed by the *dantzariak* of the different centers.

The following year, before a military coup took place in Argentina, the composer moved to New York. On her arrival, she became aware of the new compositional techniques of Augusto Novaro, a Mexican composer and author of a treatise entitled *Teorías de la Música Base del Sistema Natural* (Theories of Music Based on the Natural System). After studying with Novaro, she applied the new system to a series of Basque dances for two pianos. The work was subsequently presented, in a version choreographed by Antonio Otza, in the Centro Vasco Americano of New York in 1931. The same work, performed by Emiliana and Mirrah Alhambra, was later presented at the New York City Hall, in a concert that received an excellent review in the *New York Times*.

Even though Emiliana had been away from home for a long time, she kept contact with her homeland both through a steady correspondence with her brother, Nestor (who kept her well informed of political events in the Basque Country and Spain), and by composing works that recalled and incorporated Basque rhythms. This commitment to her homeland can be seen clearly in the song *Duérmete niña bonita* (Sleep Pretty Girl), written in celebration of the 1931 installation of the republic (also known as *niña bonita)* in Spain. Other songs from this period include: *When the Orange Blossom Time Comes Back Again* and *Yumiri* (Impression of Cuba), with texts by Ellen McGrath de Glaban; *Jota Baska* (Basque *Jota,* or dance) for four voices, with lyrics by the composer; and *Bakartasun* (Solitude) for eight voices, *txistu,* and *tamboril.* On December 15, 1931, a concert at the Roerich Museum featured songs by Emiliana with lyrics by Spanish poets such as Federico García Lorca and Antonio Machado, as well as the founder of Basque nationalism, Sabino Arana Goiri, being interpreted by Laura Mollenauer (soprano) and Luis Zamudio (baritone). Furthermore, at the same event another of Novaro's students, the pianist Esperanza Pulido, "Esperanzita," performed two sonatinas composed by Emiliana in Novaro's system.

In 1932 Emiliana went to the Caribbean, where she worked with the Centro Vasco, the Sociedad Pro Arte Musical, the Orfeón Vasco, and the soprano Angelina Torre de Damborenea. At the Teatro Auditorium of Havana, the composer presented a concert in three parts: the first featured works from her Parisian years together with songs and lyrics by Hispano-American poets. In the second part her works for piano solo were performed, and the final section featured the Orfeón Vasco. Emiliana received a praising review in the *Pro Arte Musical,* where the critic remarked: "Zubeldia tiene la noble ambición de llegar a los públicos por el camino de la verdad" (Zubeldia has the noble ambition to reach the public by the way of the truth). [36] On March 15 and 16 the composer presented a lecture entitled "La Asociación de la Música con la Poesía" (The Relationship between Music and Poetry), where she commented on her experience of working with renowned poets, remarking that "Una poesía sin música es un molino sin agua" (A poetic text without music is like a mill without water) and that "La Música, es ante todo, arte expresivo en el tiempo" (Music is, above all, an expressive art through time). [37] In June 1932 she received a standing ovation while conducting the premiere of her *Poemas Sinfónicos*

---

36 In Leticia T. Varela-Ruiz, *Maestra Maitea* ([Hermosillo]: Pro Musica de Hermosillo, [1992]), pp. 106-7.

37 Ibid, p.108.

(Symphonic Poems), in a concert with the Havana Philhar-
monic Orchestra at the Gran Teatro Nacional.

After this successful stay in the Caribbean, the following
year she traveled to Mexico where she gave several presentations of Augusto Novaro's compositional techniques, illus-
trating them with her own works. Thereafter, on returning to
New York she started to host a program at the MGM Radio
City Music Hall on Basque music — both classical and folk —
featuring many renowned artists such as Nicanor Zabaleta
and Andres Segovia. To them, Emiliana dedicated, respectively, the works *Paisaje desde el Pirineo* (Countryside from the
Pyrenees) and *Paisaje Basko* (Basque Countryside).

Between 1935 and 1936 Emiliana journeyed once more
to the Caribbean, returning to New York the following year.
On returning she learned of the tragic reality of the Spanish
Civil War, which would directly affect her family. In 1937, her
brother Alejo and her sister Eladia were imprisoned, while another brother, Friar Gumersindo, went to Zaragoza as an in-
mate sentenced to death row. Even though the composer was
deeply saddened by the news, she kept working, even moving
to Mexico in order to collaborate more closely with Novaro.
There, they spent two years preparing new compositions on
his technique, even building a piano better suited to his scale
system. [38] The instrument was subsequently first used in
1939, during one of Emiliana's presentations. However, her
promising performing career was suddenly cut short by an accident in which she seriously injured an arm. She would never
recover her former vitality in live performance, but she made
up for this loss by getting deeply involved in the intellectual
and artistic life of her new country.

Indeed, Mexico was at that time one of the most attractive
places for the thousands of people seeking refuge from the un-

---

38   The piano tuning was based on the principle of natural harmonics,
instead of the diatonic division of the octave.

stable political situation of 1930s Europe. In 1939 alone, for example, more than five thousand refugees arrived in Mexico, among them many writers, painters, and musicians. Emiliana quickly found herself meeting figures like Rodolfo Halffter and Dr. Adolfo Salazar, both frequent visitors to Novaro's house and the Instituto Francés de América Latina. They held *tertulias* (social meetings) that lasted for many hours. It was during that time of cultural effervescence that Emiliana composed pieces such as the *20 Estudios para piano.*

In 1939 the composer suffered another trauma with the death of her sister, Eladia. After experiencing terrible moments of sadness, she composed the *Sinfonía Elegíaca, a la memoria de mi hermana Eladia* (Elegiac Symphony, to the Memory of My Sister Eladia). The work was premiered many years later by the Orquesta Sinfonica de la Universidad National Autonoma de Mexico, when Emiliana received the national prize for composition in 1956.

In 1942, the composer received permission to become a permanent resident of Mexico. Five years later, the president of the University of Sonora, Prof. Manuel Quiroz Martínez, invited her to take a position at the institution as director of the Alma Mater Choir. After ten years in Mexico, Emiliana had finally found a permanent position and would remain in Hermosillo for the rest of her life. Even though her duties concerned the integration of the student choirs, she quickly started to teach piano, as well as theory and music history classes. During her academic period she would also organize lectures and concerts by guest artists and intellectuals. In 1949, during the First Congress of Secondary Schools, she presented a lecture at the University of Sonora and in 1950, the choir gave an important concert, in which songs such as *Con Amores la de mi Madre* (With the Love of My Mother) by the Basque composer Juan de Anchieta, were presented. That same year she was named director of choral groups.

Emiliana continued her educational efforts, founding several associations — such as the Sociedad de Amigos del Estudiante — that provided scholarships for poorer students. In this active way, she acted not only as a teacher, advisor, and friend, but also as a bridge between the students and the outside world, inviting renowned musicians to Hermosillo and sending local musicians to undertake graduate studies in Mexico City, the United States, and Germany. She also created a dormitory for students who had no resources, a place that was built with money earned through a series of concerts. These concerts were soon to spread beyond the borders of Sonora, being presented in Oaxaca, Mexico City, and Phoenix (Arizona), always receiving noteworthy reviews.

At the same time Emiliana's first teacher and beloved brother, Nestor, was broadcasting a program on Pamplona's Radio Requeté, where he discussed philosophical questions on music, mainly based on Emiliana's and his own ideas. Suddenly, however, he was taken seriously ill and Emiliana, after many years far away from home, decided to return to the Basque Country to visit her brother. She stayed for a month, although she never left the family house during that time. On returning to Mexico, she discovered that Novaro was also seriously ill. He died soon after, leaving all his compositions under the name Novaro-Zubeldia. Thereafter, her brother's health deteriorated yet further and in 1963 she received the news of his death. Although seriously affected by all this suffering, Emiliana never renounced her professional career, and, that same year, received a medal from the president of the university.

During the 1960s she witnessed the continuous growth of the university music department, with the moving of the Orquesta Sinfónica del Noroeste to Sonora, and the founding of a guitar department at the school. In 1968 Emiliana composed *Misa de la Asunción* (Assumption Mass), which was performed by the University of Sonora's choir in Mexico City's Palacio de Bellas Artes. Emiliana went on another concert tour with the choir in 1972, which resulted in a recording by CBS. That same year, Emiliana's only remaining brother, Martin, died.

Typically, she kept working despite all adversities and, in 1976, received the homage of her students. That year she appeared on television conducting the choir. She also learned of her husband's death. Emiliana remained active as a pedagogue and conductor until 1986, when an accident confined her to a wheelchair. In 1987 she underwent surgery but it was ultimately unsuccessful and on May 26, she died. Her funeral mass was celebrated with honors at the Catedral de la Asunción. Still remembered and admired nowadays as a talented composer and teacher, besides being a courageous and determined woman, Emiliana left a legacy of one hundred fifty-nine compositions (many of them closely related to the Basque Country), two recordings with the choir, and as many as six hundred pupils.

Berengaria of Navarre: Medieval Role Model

Rachel Bard

Unsung and almost forgotten today, Berengaria of Navarre led a life that began in obscurity, briefly shone in the fierce light that beats upon the throne, and ended in the warm glow of the love and respect of her adopted people. In many ways a woman ahead of her time, she learned how to survive her adversities and overcome her adversaries. She practiced forbearance and forgiveness during her ill-starred marriage to Richard I of England; acquired self-reliance after his death; and finally demonstrated administrative skills and wise governance as Dame of Le Mans.

Few have heard of this twelfth-century princess, daughter of Sancho VI of Navarre, who left her native land in 1191 never to return. Though she was wed to the Lionheart, greatest hero of his age, she never saw the England over which he ruled and of which she was queen. She is cursorily mentioned in English histories as Richard's wife, the implication being that she is not memorable because she bore him no children. [39]

Yet her story is worth telling. It reveals an early example of a determined woman who made her way in a man's world. Though her "liberation" was not of her choosing, she never pled the excuse of weak womanhood and rose to every challenge. She may also be seen as an embodiment of the tradi-

---

39   She fares a little better at the hands of Agnes Strickland. In her multivolume account of all the English queens, she allots 21 pages to the chapter on Berengaria. But two-thirds of the biography is devoted to Eleanor of Aquitaine and Richard. Agnes Strickland, *Lives of the Queens of England* (London, 1857), vol. 1, pp. 203-224.

tional Basque virtues of tenacity, self-respect and probity.

After seven centuries of oblivion, the verifiable facts of her childhood and young womanhood are few. During her eight-year marriage, because of the star quality of her husband, her movements are better known. Thanks to the zeal of a nineteenth-century French scholar in Le Mans, Henri Chardon, her later years were well documented.

The Young Princess

Berengaria was born about 1165, one of the five children of Sancho VI of Navarre, also known as Sancho el Sabio ("The Wise"). Her mother was Sancha, daughter of Alfonso VII of Castile. Her older brother was the Sancho who later ruled Navarre as Sancho VII, El Fuerte ("The Strong"). Her younger sister was Blanca, later Countess Blanche of Champagne.

Berengaria's childhood coincided with a relatively peaceful era for Navarre. Her father was a prudent ruler who left his kingdom considerably larger, more stable and more influential than it was when he inherited it in 1150 from his father, Garcií Ramírez IV. It included present-day Navarre, Alava, Vizcaya, Guipúzcoa and Nájera. Although Sancho had frequent disputes with his bellicose neighbors, Castile and Aragon, most of his battles were to protect his borders, not to enlarge his kingdom.[40] Berengaria probably grew up in the royal palace in Estella, with frequent visits to that of Tudela. Sancho did not have his own residence in Pamplona until 1189. Her example was a father who improved and safeguarded the Pilgrims' Route to Santiago de Compostela, founded monasteries and encouraged scholarship, and broadened the liberties of his subjects.[41] His reputation for wisdom, according

40 Angel de Apraiz, "La Significación de Sancho el Sabio en la Vida Vasca," *Vida Vasca*, 1951, p. 66.

41 Ibid., pp. 67-70.

to the historian José María LaCarra, lay chiefly in three areas: his legislative achievements — he granted *fueros* to Vitoria, Durango and other cities and created new *barrios* in Estella and Pamplona; the economic well-being his subjects enjoyed; and his political skills in keeping his country intact. [42]

The young princess had leisure time and was encouraged to learn to read and write and to appreciate poetry and music, especially that of the Provençal troubadours who frequented the courts of Europe. One of the most renowned of these troubadours was Prince Richard, son of King Henry II of England and Eleanor of Aquitaine, his queen. But Berengaria's first impression of Richard was not as a musician, but as a redoubtable jouster. When she was only ten or eleven, he came to visit her older brother Sancho and take part in a tournament in Pamplona. It would make a pretty story to relate that the young prince and princess fell in love at first sight. Some of the medieval chroniclers, as well as several novelists, have told such a tale. But in all likelihood they regarded each other with polite indifference. Berengaria was too young, and Richard, who would have been about fifteen, was more interested in horsemanship, hunting and mock battles than romance.

Only some fifteen years later, when Richard had just succeeded to the throne, was the subject of marriage between the two broached. Eleanor suggested it to Sancho VI, for political reasons. She worried about protection of the far-flung Anglo-French borders, especially in her beloved Aquitaine where the count of Toulouse was a frequent threat. She knew that England needed an ally in that region. She saw how useful a friend Navarre could be, since its territories north of the Pyrenees bordered Aquitaine. But for the time being, there was no final agreement between Eleanor and Sancho.

---

42 José María LaCarra, *Historia Política del Reino de Navarra desde sus Orígenes hasta su Incorporación a Castilla* (Pamplona, 1972), vol. 3, pp. 86-87.

Then in 1190 Richard announced that he was planning to go to Palestine. Jerusalem was held by the Saracens, and good Christians burned to recover it. With bravado and enthusiasm, Richard decided to lead a Crusade. It would be a path to glory as well as an opportunity for enrichment. [43]

This intensified Eleanor's concerns. What if Richard were to die in the Holy Land without an heir? It was vital that he marry. She thought again of the Navarrese princess. With characteristic decisiveness, Eleanor traveled to Pamplona to arrange the marriage, and found Sancho agreeable. His daughter was twenty-four, and so far no suitable fiancé had come forward from the eligible royalty of the Iberian Peninsula. Richard was more than suitable — he was handsome, a renowned warrior, and the ruler of a kingdom that stretched from the British Isles to the Pyrenees and included more of France than the king of France himself could lay claim to. Sancho saw the alliance as a plum for Navarre. We do not know what Berengaria thought. We only know that soon after Eleanor's arrival the two women began their travels across the Pyrenees and through France, intending to rendezvous with Richard before he set sail for the Holy Land.

Yet there was one obstacle, which was soon to threaten not only the marriage but the very Crusade. Years before, Henry II and King Louis VII of France had agreed to the betrothal of their children: fourteen-year-old Richard and nine-year-old Alice. The betrothal was meant to impart a measure of stability to the volatile English-French relations, and for some years it had been useful. Now that Louis' son Philip was king, and he and Richard were to be partners in the Crusade, the alliance was vital. While the two monarchs were preparing to embark from Messina in Sicily, Philip insisted that Richard honor the agreement. Richard refused, on the grounds that Alice had been his father's mistress. [44]

---

43   John Gillingham, *Richard the Lionheart* (New York, 1978), p. 142.

44   Amy Kelly, *Eleanor of Aquitaine and the Four Kings* (Cambridge, Mas-

When Eleanor shortly arrived with Berengaria, it was too much for Philip. Furious at the spurning of his sister, he left hastily for Palestine. It was the beginning of the enmity between Richard and Philip that was to later imperil the progress of the Crusade.

And the field was left to Berengaria.

The chronicler Ambrose reported on Richard's joy at his fiancée's arrival: "Most dear did the King love her and revere." But Ambrose was probably writing what his public would want to hear. His description of the princess was not so effulgent: "A prudent maid, a gentle lady, virtuous and fair, neither false nor double-tongued." [45]

Richard now gave the first sign that he lacked enthusiasm for the union. He argued for postponement because Lent was about to begin, and festivities would be unseemly. Eleanor departed, having done all she could to assure the marriage and the succession. She left Berengaria in the care of her daughter Joanna, recentiy widowed queen of Sicily.

On April 10, 1191, Richard gave the order to sail. Berengaria and Joanna and their ladies were assigned to a dromond — slower and more ponderous than the galleys of Richard and his warriors, but safer. A great storm arose and scattered the fleet of some 200 vessels. The dromond, out of contact with the others, eventually arrived off the coast of Cyprus and took shelter at Limassol harbor. To add to their worries about the whereabouts of Richard and the rest of the fleet, the captain and his royal charges did not trust the self-styled emperor of Cyprus, Isaac Comnenus. He sent boats out and tried to lure them ashore with promises of fine food and Cyp-riot

sachusetts, 1950), p. 263.

45   E. N. Stone, tr., *Three Old French Chronicles of the Crusades;* Ambrose, *L'Estoire de la guerre sainte;* Robert of Cleri, *L'Estoire de chiaus que conquisent Constantinope;* Minstrel de Reims, *La Chronique de Reims* (Seattle, 1939), p. 26.

wine, but they suspected he hoped to hold them for ransom. The captain turned about and made for the open ocean.

Just then, Richard's ship and the rest of the fleet made their way into harbor. When he realized the situation, Richard was so angry that he attacked the Cypriots, driving Isaac into the hills. But before the final assault, Richard was persuaded by his counselors that the marriage could wait no longer, "if only out of regard for the bride's reputation," wrote the chronicler.[46] Besides, a party of knights had just arrived from Palestine, whose presence would add lustre to the event. So Richard postponed his pursuit of Isaac long enough for the ceremony, which was held in Limassol on May 12, 1191.

Queen Berengaria

Richard's dazzling raiment is described by the chroniclers in meticulous detail, down to the last silken tunic. But they do not tell us what Berengaria wore. Her effigy at LeMans may give us a clue, because it seems to show her as a bride. Her hair is loose and unbound as would befit a bride but not a wife or widow. Her veil is caught with a jeweled crown and her flowing tunic is confined with a jeweled girdle.

After the marriage service Richard was crowned king of Cyprus (he had already been crowned king of England, at Westminster Abbey in 1189). With equal ceremony, Berengaria was crowned queen of England and Cyprus. Feasting followed and then Richard and his army sallied forth to seek out and capture Isaac. They succeeded in short order.

Now, it was on to Palestine and the real purpose of the expedition: to drive the infidels out of the Holy City of Jerusalem. Berengaria and Joanna sailed in the dromond as before. But this time there were no disasters, and the entire fleet

---

46   Richard of Devizes, *Chronicle*, Richard Howlett, ed. (Rolls Series 82, III).

landed safely at St-Jean d'Acre. They found Philip of France and the third partner in the Crusade, Leopold of Austria, impatiently awaiting Richard and his aid in their assault on St-Jean. After the capture of the city on July 12, Berengaria and Joanna were installed in the city's royal palace, where they remained for most of the following year. We are told that they spent their time on embroidery and other fancy-work, and that "they held each other dear, and lived as doves in a cage." [47] But they must have found their life confining, and welcomed the diversion of a journey south to Jaffa, where Richard was preparing for the assault on Jerusalem.

Observers noted Richard's growing coolness toward Berengaria and there is no evidence that they spent any time together as man and wife. Some later writers suggested that he had lost his heart to another — perhaps the daughter of Isaac, whom he had taken under his protection after her father was incarcerated. But the contemporary chroniclers say only that he was far too busy with his battles to devote himself to his queen.

For the rest of 1191 and until September 1192 the Crusaders marched about Palestine, battling the Saracens and their adroit leader Saladin. But capture of Jerusalem proved a chimera. Saladin was firmly in control and his troops far outnumbered the Crusaders. He had laid waste all the surrounding countryside so the Christians could find no food or provisions. And he had poisoned the wells. To add to the difficulties, Philip, still harboring resentment of Richard, lost enthusiasm for the venture and with many of his troops returned to France. Bereft of this support and realizing how suicidal an assault would be, Richard signed a truce with Saladin in the autumn of 1192, and the inconclusive Third Crusade petered out.

---

47   Pierre de Langtoft, *Chronicle,* Thomas Wright, ed. (Rolls Series 47), vol. 2, p. 49.

Richard dispatched his wife and his sister to France on September 29, 1192. It was to be three years before Berengaria saw him again. His adventures during this period are well known and the stuff of legend. Hers are a matter of conjecture. We do know that she and Joanna made their way to Rome and sheltered for a time under the protection of Pope Celestine. They went to Marseilles and from there were accompanied by Alfonso II of Aragon through Provence. For the final leg of the journey, Raymond of St-Gilles, son of the count of Toulouse, conducted them to Poitiers, where Eleanor had a palace. Joanna subsequently married Raymond.

Back in France, Berengaria vanished from public life. Eleanor had by now given up any hope that the marriage would produce an heir, and though the unhappy queen was permitted to lodge in the Angevin palaces, she was largely ignored by her royal in-laws.

Meanwhile all Europe's attention was riveted on the fate of Richard. For months his whereabouts were a mystery; he had not been heard of since leaving St-Jean d'Acre. Then word came that on his way back from the Holy Land he had been imprisoned by his erstwhile ally, Leopold of Austria, and then by Leopold's lord, Henry VI of Germany. Henry demanded a huge ransom, which Eleanor managed to raise. As soon as he was freed Richard went straight to England without visiting his queen. He was recrowned at Winchester Cathedral on April 16, 1194. Eleanor occupied the place of honor opposite him, but Berengaria was not invited.

Richard soon returned to France to reassert his authority, which had suffered from Philip's aggressions. But still he made no effort to see Berengaria. In fact, rumor had it that he was devoting himself to evil companions, to such an extent that he was reprimanded by the Church. A righteous hermit warned him that he ran the risk of eternal damnation unlesss he mended his ways and returned to his queen.

Yet he continued to ignore her, until a severe illness nearly cost him his life. Fearful of the retribution threatened by
the hermit, he publicly repented and rejoined Berengaria for
Christmas at Poitiers in 1195. But the reconciliation did not
last long. If Berengaria harbored hopes for a normal wedded
life at last, they were dashed when Richard abruptly left, to
resume his battles with Philip.

For the next two years his one true love was a huge castle,
Château Gaillard, which he was building in Normandy. He
meant it to be fit to withstand the worst Philip could throw
against it. He called it his "daughter." He had clearly given up
any hope that his marriage might be fruitful.

We will never know why it was not. Perhaps Berengaria
could not bear children. This is more likely than the common tale that Richard's alleged homosexuality was to blame.
He had, after all, according to many accounts, fathered one
illegitimate son before his marriage.[48] And he knew the importance of the succession. At any rate, in 1196 he formally
repudiated Berengaria and acknowledged his brother John as
his heir. Berengaria retired to an obscure castle near Angers,
possibly at Beaufort-en-Vallée. There she received the news of
Richard's death in 1199, brought by Hugh, Bishop of Lincoln,
who was on his way to the funeral.

Aggressive to the end, Richard had besieged the castle of
a rebellious vassal and died when a wound from an arrow fes-
tered. He was forty-two. Before he died he repented his sins
and took the Holy Sacrament — for the first time since his fit
of penitence three years before.

Eleanor was at his deathbed, and at his funeral at Fontevrault Abbey. But Berengaria, though within a day's journey,
was summoned to neither. The Bishop of Lincoln urged her
to come with him but she declined. However, when Eleanor

---

48   Anthony Bridge, *Richard the Lionheart* (New York, 1989), p. 141.

held a memorial service at Fontevrault Abbey a few months later and invited Berengaria, she did attend.

The Widowed Queen

Did Berengaria mourn her husband? We do not know. Publicly, she was loyal to his memory for the rest of her life, wearing the white of a widow whenever she went out and signing herself as Queen of England. In 1209, after she became Dame of Le Mans, she gave one of the city's abbeys a vineyard, in honor of the anniversary of Richard's birth. [49] But her loyalty to his successors was sorely tried. For two decades after his death her life centered on her efforts to obtain her rightful share of Richard's estate and her own dowry, the extensive lands assigned to her by her marriage settlement. King John was her most stubborn and wily adversary. He promised much and delivered nothing. At least once he offered her a safe-conduct to England, where they might discuss the matter in person. But she refused, suspecting a ruse; after all, had not his father imprisoned his mother for fourteen years, to keep her from interfering in the affairs of the kingdom?

Fortunately, she found a champion in Pope Innocent III and another in his successor, Pope Honorius III. The Church had a tradition of protecting widows and orphans, and if their enemies were royal so much the better. Such cases gave the Pope a highly visible opportunity to demonstrate the primacy of the Church vis-a-vis temporal power. The rivalry of the two authorities for men's hearts, minds and money had become spirited by the thirteenth century.

For twenty long years, however, Berengaria's efforts would be unavailing. After papal threats to John and even an excommunication, the Pope would prevail in 1220, and

---

49   Henri Chardon, *Histoire de la Reine Bérengère, Femme de Richard Coeur-de-Lion et Dame Douairière du Mans* (Le Mans, 1866), p. 395. Chardon is the source of most of the story of Berengaria's life after 1204.

Berengaria would receive a pension from England — but not from King John. By that time he would be dead and his son Henry III would accede.

Meanwhile she had at last found a secure abode. For a few years she had taken refuge with her sister Blanche, countess of Champagne. Then in 1204 when Eleanor of Aquitaine died, at the astonishing age of eighty-two, Philip of France made haste to seize her lands in France. Berengaria was outraged and went to see Philip and assert herself. She claimed that many of these cities and dominions were rightfully hers; Richard had been duke of Aquitaine, and after his mother's death she was the heir. She relinquished her claims when Philip gave her the city of Le Mans in exchange for certain of the disputed properties. His motives may not have been disinterested. With Berengaria ensconced in Le Mans as his vassal, the Plantagenets would be unlikely to attack it in their ongoing efforts to reclaim their lost lands in France. And since the gift was only for her lifetime, it would revert to the French crown at her death.

Dame of the City

As Dame of Le Mans, Berengaria had to learn new skills, at which she succeeded admirably. She learned the arts of governance, and her people respected and admired her. She had to learn diplomacy and even deviousness, because of her running battle with the bishop and chapter of St. Julien's Cathedral. The churchmen were accustomed to more freedom to tax and administer justice in Le Mans than Berengaria thought proper. Especially after the naming of Maurice as bishop of Le Mans in 1216, the disputes over the limits of civil vs. ecclesiastical power became more frequent and acrimonious.

One incident will illustrate the vehemence of both sides. In 1217, a certain Julien Laurent, one of her bailiffs, had collected a tax on animals sold in a section of the city between the area governed by the cathedral chapter and that by her administration. It was an area long in dispute. The canons of the chapter demanded that Laurent yield them the money — a matter of only five farthings. When he refused he was excommunicated. The canons asked Berengaria to force him to hand over the money. She would not, maintaining that the area where he had collected it was within her fief. The chapter then placed the entire city and its churches under an interdiction. This meant that no churches could hold services, not a Mass could be held, not a marriage consecrated, not a body be given a Christian burial.

Refusing to live in a city where she could not attend holy services, even in her own private chapel, Berengaria left. The interdiction lasted for eighteen months and the people were in despair. Finally the queen's counselors persuaded the chapter to offer to lift the interdiction if Berengaria would return; for the moment, nothing was said about the five farthings. She did return, and was met with considerable ceremony by the chapter — not only out of honor to her, but also in the hope of getting their money — a paltry sum, but receiving it would vindicate their position, Chardon surmises.[50]

However, the affair dragged on for two more years. Berengaria continued to maintain her rights and placed her case before a papal legate, who conferred at length with his colleagues, considering the parties' rights and the principles involved. Their judgement: the money should go to the chapter. By now tempers had cooled and all sides were relieved to have the matter ended. And nobody was happier than Julien Laurent, who was cleared of all charges.

There were more controversies, but none were documented after 1223 so peace or at least a truce must have been declared. Now Berengaria was free to devote herself more sin-

---

50   Ibid, p. 438.

glemindedly to good works. Like other rulers, she may have given more thought, as she aged, to how history would see her. She took great interest in the Cathedral of St-Julien, and initiated the construction of its *arcsboutants* — possibly the first flying buttresses in France. She contributed to construction and repair of other churches in the city. Throughout her residence in Le Mans she took special interest in the welfare of her own chapel, St-Pierre-la-Cour.

One of her ambitions had been to found a Cistercian abbey as her father and mother had done. The young Louis IX had just ascended the throne of France, and she asked him for help. With the advice or at least consent of his mother, the queen regent Blanche of Castile, he gave her a plot of land outside the city, on the River Huisne. Here, in 1229, began the construction of the Abbe de la Piété-Dieu d'Épau. Berengaria followed progress of the work carefully, and augmented it constantly. She acquired lands surrounding the abbey to add to what King Louis had given her. She bought nearby vineyards to add to the abbey's money-making resources.

Chardon tells a charming story to illustrate the queen's attention to detail. He does not vouch for the truth but, he says, it has the merit of "bringing a smile to our lips, which has not been possible up to now in view of the sorrowful events that filled her tormented life." The tale goes that a mill on the river was so noisy that it greatly annoyed the monks who were working nearby and they complained to the queen. One of her counselors advised her: "Buy the mill, and give it to the monks. Then every time they hear the noisy wheel turning, they will be full of joy because it means coins falling in their coffers." She followed the advice, and the monks were appeased. [51]

All was going well: the walls of the abbey were rising rapidly, the Cistercian monks who were to inhabit it were on

---

51   Ibid, p. 461.

their way from Clteaux, and the dedication had been scheduled. Then queen Berengaria died, Dec. 23, 1230, aged 65. Instead of being welcomed by their benefactress, the white-robed monks prayed at her tomb in the new abbey. As she would have wished, work went on, and the completed abbey, with its church, chapter house, dortoir and scriptorium was dedicated by Geoffrey, Bishop of Le Mans, in 1234.

For six centuries, Berengaria's effigy was displayed in the abbey, and the people of Le Mans visited it to pay homage to their Dame. Later it was moved to the cathedral of Le Mans, and in 1921 was moved with great pomp from the south to the north transept. After the ceremony the cathedral organ played the national anthem of England. Berengaria's effigy is regal in pose and costume. She wears a long robe, fastened at the neck with an ornate clasp. From her girdle, studded with precious stones, hangs a purse. Her head rests on a cushion and her hair is pardy covered with a veil. She wears the massive crown of the queen of England. The face is that of a conventionally attractive, if not beautiful, woman. In her hands is a book, showing a portrait of herself flanked by two torches, as though on a bier.

The epitaph reads:

> Homage to Berengaria of Navarre, queen of England and of Cyprus, our good Lady of Le Mans… To the sovereign majesty, beauty and goodness and the virtues of her youth, were added her greatness in adversity and her resignation in sacrifice. Queen, in this sanctified place, may your venerated remains rest in perpetual peace.

The abbey is about a mile and a half from the town center, and when built was surrounded by forests and farms. Today it is still in the midst of verdure, and the River Huisne still flows quietly past its boundaries. It is beautifully preserved, thanks to the French Ministry of Fine Arts. Though Cistercian monks no longer live there, it is a center of learning and culture and the site of gatherings the year around.

Cast involuntarily as a player on Europe's royal chessboard, denied her rightful place as queen of England, Berengaria still made her mark and left as her legacy not only the abbey, but the respect and love of the people of Le Mans, which endure to this day.

Becoming Basque: The Euskarapen of Raymonde and Claire Noblia

Maggi Nicholson

Introduction

"Tell our story," said Claire Noblia. She and her mother were not born Basques, but rather chose to become Basque, a process referred to in Euskara as *euskarapen*. Over the course of half a century their exploration of this process followed parallel paths, and yet each experience was unique. Claire Noblia hopes that the details of their lives will encourage Basque women who were born to their heritage to embrace it, regardless of their age. To that end, Claire generously provided the information reported here. I am deeply grateful for her patience in answering my questions, for her warm friendship, and for her gracious hospitality over the years.

Becoming Basque

Raymonde Richard Noblia and her daughter Claire represent a pattern of modern Basque female experience that is not often described. Although they were both born in Iparralde, the region of the Basque Country north of the Pyrenees, they did not learn the Basque language, Euskara, as their first language. Nor did they receive any early childhood instruction in being Basque. Instead, they each made the conscious decision to embrace Basqueness later in life.

Raymonde made her decision in her late twenties, after marrying a Basque and giving birth to Claire. As Claire approached adolescence, she followed her mother's example. They both studied Euskara and attended classes about Basque customs. They also both became involved in *euskalgintza* or Basque cultural activity, a decision that implied a commitment to taking part in and encouraging events and acts that promoted Basque culture.

The success of their transition to Basqueness was such that those who meet Raymonde often think she was born Basque. When daughter Claire showed me the extensive Noblia and Richard family tree drawn by Raymonde on a three-foot by four-foot poster board, I saw that the Noblia side was dominated by Basque family names through the lineages of husband Felix Noblia's six great grandparents. In sharp contrast, none of Raymonde's great grandparents had a clearly Basque name. Nevertheless, after twenty years of genealogical research, Raymonde did find a number of Basques or *euskaldunak* among her eighteenth-century ancestors.

Raymonde's Early Years

The details of Raymonde's youth, including her first years of marriage, are critical to an understanding of both her choice of cultural identification and her diligence in pursuing her commitment to becoming Basque. She was intelligent and was trained in an academic setting available to few women of her generation. The strong personality of her earliest years was tempered by the challenges she would face in her twenties. Long before she discovered that she possessed Basque ancestors, she exhibited *indarra* (strength and endurance) and *sendotasuna* (courage and fortitude), both qualities that have been traditionally admired by the Basques.[52]

---

52   These concepts are particularly important in Basque culture. See Sandra Ott, *The Circle of Mountains: A Basque Shepherding Community*

Raymonde's early orientation was strongly scientific. Born in the French Basque city of Bayonne (Baiona in
Basque), in 1916, she was the second of three children and the
only daughter of Joseph Richard, a practicing physician with
non-Basque forebears from Agen and Thouars. Her mother
Madeleine was the daughter of Albert Toucoulat, a physician
whose paternal ancestors had lived in Gan, just south of Pau,
to the east of the Basque Country in Béarn. Madeleine's sister also married a doctor. Raymonde's older brother Claude
became an engineer, and her younger brother, Pierre, who
studied medicine, became a radiologist. Raymonde attended
local schools in Bayonne, including a co-educational *lycée* or
high school. She was an enthusiastic tennis player, and was
also the female swimming champion of the Basque coast in
her teens. After a preparatory year in the Faculty of Sciences
at the University of Bordeaux, Raymonde began her medical
studies in Paris in 1934 and by June 1939, she had completed
all her medical courses.

Meanwhile, Raymonde had fallen in love with an officer
in the air force, but he was not interested in marriage. Even
so, after medical school Raymonde returned to Bayonne to
prepare for her wedding, to be held late in August 1939. Although the man of her dreams did not want to marry her, all
women in her family's social circle were expected to marry, so
she had accepted the fiancé, Felix Noblia, whom her parents
had chosen for her. They had been advised, in turn, by the
chaplain of their sons' secondary school. He informed them
about former student Noblia who was now sufficiently established in his career to consider marriage. Raymonde had met

(1981; reprint, Reno, Las Vegas and London: University of Nevada
Press, 1993), pp. 29, 55, 87-88, 144, 153; Sandra Ott, "*Indarra:* Some
Reflections on a Basque Concept," in J.G. Peristiany and Julian Pitt-
Rivers, eds. *Honor and Grace in Anthropology* (Cambridge, New York, Port
Chester, Melbourne and Sydney: Cambridge University Press, 1992),
pp. 193-214; and Joseba Zulaika, *Basque Violence: Metaphor and Sacrament*
(Reno and Las Vegas: University of Nevada Press, 1988), pp. 328-31.

Noblia, since he attended her brothers' school, but she had had little opportunity to get to know him because he lived in the French Ivory Coast colony.

Felix Noblia, a thirty-three-year-old Basque, was the youngest of five sons born to a family of chocolate manufacturers who lived near Bayonne. He spent several years in training as a medical officer, and was then employed on ocean liners during 1930 and 1931. He entered the French army in 1932 where he served again as a medical officer and the army sent him to the Ivory Coast colony where he was based in the inland town of Abengourou. While there, he bought and improved a local dispensary that he would operate until his death in 1984. In the mid-1930s, Felix also began acting as his family's intermediary for buying and transporting the cacao beans essential to their business. He soon realized the economic wisdom of renting a cacao plantation, where he made his home and subsequently purchased the plantation. When he returned to Bayonne to visit his parents in 1939, he was indeed well established in business in West Africa. With his future secure, it was only natural for him to entertain his old chaplain's suggestion that he consider marriage with Raymonde Richard, a woman with a lively personality and shared interests, since she also had studied medicine. They were thus married.

Raymonde and Felix traveled to Spain on their honeymoon but less than a week later, on September 3, 1939, Britain and France declared war against Germany. The two newlyweds returned at once to Bayonne so that Felix could depart without delay for the Ivory Coast where, he believed, he would be recalled into service by the army. In the meantime Raymonde stayed with her parents and occasionally helped her father with his practice. Indeed, when he once fell ill with a severe case of pneumonia, she assumed all his medical responsibilities throughout the period of his illness and subsequent recuperation. That was to be the only time she would practice medicine outside her family circle.

Nevertheless, in January 1940, she went to Paris to take her clinical exams in internal medicine, surgery, and obstetrics. She returned to Paris again in late February to have her thesis typed before presenting it to the medical jury on March 6 as the last requirement for her medical degree. She wrote the thesis on tachycardia paroxystic, an episodic rapid heart beat with which her mother had been afflicted. By the end of March, she returned to Iparralde and moved into a house called "Loreduna" (full of flowers), a wedding present from her father, in Anglet (Angelu). At the same time, however, she also began saying farewell to her family and friends for she was planning to join Felix in West Africa.

A New Home

Raymonde kept a small calendar in her purse. In April 1940, in addition to her social engagements, she began jotting down details of ships that might take her to West Africa. Three different sailings were cancelled, and she dutifully noted these events in the calendar. At last, on May 8, she departed by train for Marseilles, boarding the ship "Bonfora" that sailed for the Ivory Coast on May 11. The ship made ports of call to exotic places during the seventeen-day voyage: Casablanca, Morocco; Dakar, Senegal; Conakry, Guinea; and Freetown, Sierra Leone. The day before the ship sailed, the German assault on France through Holland and Belgium began. Thus while Raymonde's thoughts were filled with the anticipation of seeing her husband, she was also naturally concerned about the war in Europe. During the voyage, she learned that Dutch military forces had surrendered to the Germans and on May 28, the very day that Raymonde reached the Ivory Coast, she heard that Belgium had capitulated. Felix was waiting for her in Port Bouet. For the first time since their honeymoon eight months before, the newlyweds were together again. They spent three nights and two days in Abidjan, the capital of the colony, where Felix introduced her to his friends and prepared for their journey inland.

On May 31, 1940 Felix and Raymonde left Abidjan and headed for Sankadiokrou and Felix's plantation. Although the distance between the two was slightly over a hundred miles as the crow flies, in reality they had to travel 150 miles on the ground to reach their destination. The trip took three days. The roads were rudimentary tracks through heavy vegetation, and every river had to be crossed by ferry. The long days of grueling travel were relieved by the warm welcomes they received on the nights of May 31 and June 1 in the homes of Felix's friends along the way.

At last Raymonde arrived at the plantation that was to be her new home but once again the war intruded. By the early summer of 1940 German troops were advancing rapidly into France. Consequently, less than a week after their arrival in Sankadiokrou, the French command mobilized their overseas armed forces. The local commander ordered Felix to report to Bouaké, and he complied, taking Raymonde with him. They drove northwest to Bouaké on June 6, 1940, but no sooner had they arrived than they were told to continue north another hundred miles. All the while Raymonde recorded their movements on her little calendar, including their arrival at Korhogo on June 11.

The Noblias stayed in Korhogo for the rest of June, awaiting further orders from the French command, along with other colonists and army personnel. Meanwhile the war in Europe raged on and the Germans, exploiting superior tactics and lightning mobility, marched into Paris on June 14. The French Prime Minister, Paul Reynaud, favored fighting on and even reorganizing the government in North Africa if necessary. However, another group headed by World War

One hero Marshal Pétain argued that France had suffered all it could and further bloodshed would only lead to the disintegration of France. Pétain subsequently formed a new government on June 16, negotiating an armistice that he signed on June 22. It divided the country into two: a Nazi occupied zone, with its capital in Paris, principally in the north but following the coastline down to the border with Spain and thus incorporating the French Basque Country; the remaining territory of France, principally in the south and with its capital in Vichy, was ruled by the collaborationist government of Pétain. [53]

By this time Raymonde had stopped jotting the defeats in her calendar. In July, from their quarters in Korhogo, they learned that the French navy had been defeated off the coast of Oran, Algeria, and they watched with dismay as the power of the Vichy government was extended to the French West African colonies. The last entry on Raymonde's little calendar was on August 1, 1940: "Demobilization!" The exclamation point indicated both relief and frustration. They were relieved that Felix would not be sent into battle, but they were frustrated at the lack of resistance offered by the overseas forces to the takeover by the collaborationist regime.

Raymonde and Felix returned to their plantation and lived there quietly for the rest of the year. Raymonde was interested in her new environment and kept herself busy complementing Felix's practical efforts at the dispensary. She didn't seem at all concerned by the fact that she was miles away from the nearest Europeans and even had a small laboratory constructed near their living quarters. It was not contiguous, however, for safety reasons. In her lab, she used a microscope to study the blood of syphilitics. Sometimes she worked late into the night by gas lantern. She also took photographs of people

53   Robert O. Paxton, *Europe in the Twentieth Century* (Fort Worth: Harcourt Brace, 1997), pp. 444-47.

suffering from leprosy, yaws, elephantiasis, and other tropical diseases, and later analyzed the photos, compiling copious notes on these disorders. Her research was put to good use as Felix applied her findings to his treatment of patients for years to come. During those last months of 1940, Raymonde also had the opportunity, at last, to become acquainted with her husband. She discovered that Felix was very shy, and that he had a fascination with the local Agni people and their distinctive customs. His observations of their rich cultures reminded him of the Basque festivals and activities of his youth. Studying the Agni's ethnic solidarity rekindled Felix's pride in his own patrimony. He was inspired to incorporate elements of his cultural heritage into his family life. His enthusiasm about being Basque impressed Raymonde, who had grown up in a family unconcerned about their cultural roots.

A Year of Crisis

Raymonde's idyllic life on the plantation lasted only a brief six months. In January of 1941, she and Felix were separated again when Felix was arrested by an official of the newly installed Vichy government of French West Africa, and transported five hundred miles away to a concentration camp in Bamako, Mali. Even though they were far from the European front, the war had again destroyed their tranquility.

Raymonde investigated her husband's arrest and discovered that Felix had been denounced to the government by someone who claimed that he listened to English radio broadcasts transmitted from Britain's Gold Coast colony just twelve miles away to the east. The fact that Felix did not understand English meant nothing to the authorities. In fact it was Raymonde who listened to the English news and translated it for her husband. But none of that mattered. She soon received official word that Felix had been condemned to death.

Raymonde decided she must plead for her husband's life. It would not be easy to journey to Dakar during wartime. The bureaucracy would be complicated, and the physical journey would be strenuous. Yet she battled her way through the requisite permissions and finally was able to begin the trip. She traveled by car and by train, westward through the interior of French West Africa. Once she reached Dakar, she had to wait for weeks for an appointment with Governor Boisson. When she finally got an audience, she made an impassioned appeal for clemency but Boisson did not seem to care. Frustrated by his lack of concern, she wrote to her influential godfather, General Philippe Maurin, and asked him to intercede on her husband's behalf. At last, Governor Boisson was convinced to commute Felix's death sentence to one of exile.

However, Raymonde's journey was not over. Once Felix's sentence was commuted, she faced another six hundred miles of grueling travel to Bamako, the location of the concentration camp. Yet she never faltered. Once reunited, they made arrangements to leave West Africa as soon as possible. They could not return to their plantation home because Felix might be arrested again. They therefore decided to head north to Algeria. This time, there would be no ship making exotic ports of call. The 1,800 miles would be covered on land. To make matters more difficult, Raymonde was now pregnant.

Ever the researcher, Raymonde continued her photographic habits for the duration of the journey. She preserved images of the local houses they passed. In Upper Volta (Burkina today), she photographed huts with conical roofs. In Algeria, she photographed adobe-walled homes. One snapshot captured Felix being carried on a porter's back through dense, boggy vegetation. Another photo showed their truck being ferried across a river on a small raft. In yet another, Raymonde and Felix are straddling two diminutive donkeys, riding along with their feet nearly touching the sand. As they crossed the

Sahara, someone snapped a picture of Raymonde standing beside three resting camels. From Bamako to the coast of Algeria, they walked, drove, ferried, and rode donkeys and camels, but at least they were together.

When they reached the Mediterranean coast, Raymonde and Felix had to part again. They knew that if he returned to France, Felix would share the fate of all the able-bodied young men in the occupied countries. He would be sent to labor on a German farm or in a German factory. Felix decided to remain in Saida, Algeria. He got a job at a grain mill, where he would work until the end of the war. But Raymonde was now six months pregnant, and they decided that she should return to France. So she continued on alone, by boat and by train, and finally reached Iparralde at the end of December 1941. She had spent the entire year traveling from one place to another. All in all, since leaving home to join him, she had traveled 4,300 miles, 2,500 of them without her husband.

They had been married for twenty-eight months and had spent only half of them together. On her return, therefore, Raymonde realized that the survival of their marriage would require something stronger than a shared interest in medicine. Felix was very proud of his Basque heritage, and Raymonde began to consider what she might do to capture and preserve some concrete element of this heritage for their offspring.

A New Path

Upon her return, Raymonde found a German officer named Carl Dieter living in her house. As part of the German occupation of the French Basque Country he had been officially billeted at Loreduna during her absence, along with an aide, and would remain there until the spring of 1944. Surprisingly, he would prove to be an unexpected catalyst for Raymonde's journey to Basqueness.

Dieter was singled out for a special intelligence assignment in southwestern France because of his extraordinary linguistic skill.[54] Besides being fluent in French, he was one of the very few Germans who knew any Euskara and to Raymonde's surprise he had an impressive facility for comprehending spoken Basque. His achievement thus clearly indicated that being raised in a Basque-speaking household was not necessarily a prerequisite for learning Euskara. His successful mastery of the difficult non-Indo-European language therefore had a strong and positive influence on Raymonde's growing decision to study her husband's natal tongue. Dieter had an additional and more immediate influence on Raymonde because he was also an avid *euskaltzale* or Bascophile. He was therefore enthusiastic about all things Basque, interested in both ancient traditions and continuing customs, and was also eager to learn more about local history and architecture. His enthusiasm for Basque culture impressed Pvaymonde and confirmed for her the intrinsic value of Felix's patrimony.

The conjunction of Dieter's positive cultural evaluation with the arrival of the child she was carrying accelerated Raymonde's decision to act despite the wartime situation. She thus decided to trace Felix's Basque lineage. This was a feasible goal since Iparralde was no longer under attack, and since her scientific training gave her a solid basis for serious genealogical research. Documenting the Noblia ancestors would tangibly demonstrate her support of Felix's cultural pride. Moreover, if Raymonde also traced her own ancestors,

---

54   As James E. Jacob observes of the German occupation of Iparralde, "since World War I Germany had shown itself willing to aid restive minorities in order to weaken its enemies, which only added to a long-standing German scholarly interest in the ethnography and linguistics of Europe's minorities," and, "some of the German officers sent to the Basque country were in fact professors of linguistics or anthropology with serious academic interests and occasionally ties with the Basques." See *Hills of Conflict: Basque Nationalism in Trance* (Reno, Las Vegas and London: University of Nevada Press, 1994), pp. 107-08, 114.

she would double the genealogical legacy for her baby. Little Claire was delivered at Loreduna on April 3, 1942, and Raymonde's own father assisted in the delivery.

Food was short in wartime France. As a result, during Claire's infancy Raymonde initiated a new scientific investigation, one that grew out of her concern about increasing food shortages. Once again, she established a home laboratory but this time she not only analyzed the nutritional properties of the cacao bean and the banana, but studied the dietary usefulness of local resources that were seldom used for food. At the same time, Raymonde began her search for Felix's and her own ancestors. She explored the municipal archives of Bayonne and other nearby towns, seeking information on the Noblia and Richard progenitors. All the while she kept Felix informed of her efforts by letters. Then, in 1943, she had the opportunity to show him her files in person when he managed a brief secret visit to Iparralde. Before he returned to Algeria, Raymonde was pregnant again. After Felix's departure, Raymonde continued her archival quest for ancestors. She took a break in 1944 when her son Francois [55] was born but was soon back at work, and continued her genealogical research until the war in Europe ended in June 1945.

Once the war was over, Raymonde decided to rejoin her husband in Africa. She left Claire and François in the care of her parents at Loreduna and sailed for the Ivory Coast. She and Felix returned to the plantation where she again pursued her medical research. In December 1946, Raymonde again returned to France to give birth to their third child, Agnès. Felix stayed behind in Africa to oversee the plantation while this time Raymonde remained in France to care for her young brood. She also took the opportunity to resume her tenacious

---

55 François "Patxi" Noblia later became a well-known Basque political and cultural activist. See Jacob, *Hills of Conflict*, pp. 151, 155-56, 277, 331.

pursuit of the family ancestors. With three children under five at home, the archives offered a welcome tranquility. She successfully traced family lines back through the nineteenth century, growing increasingly adept at deciphering older and older records, despite difficult penmanship and fading ink on the documents.

In the late 1940s, Raymonde entered a new phase of becoming Basque when she began to study Euskara. By now she understood the importance of that unique language to Basque identity, and began private lessons with Pierre Oyhamburu. Her medical studies and scientific research had prepared her well in the areas of concentration and discipline and she made excellent progress, even after the birth of her fourth child, Kattalin, in 1949. By this time, Claire was seven years old. She remembers that while her mother spoke very little in Basque she generally understood a great deal of other people's conversations. In 1951, however, when Raymonde's fifth child, Laurent, was born, her command of written Euskara was sufficient to allow her to supervise her older children's use of Basque in their letters to their father whenever he was overseeing the Ivory Coast plantation.

During the 1950s, Raymonde increased her level of Basque activities to those she could share with her children. She created a large map on a wall of their summer home in Cambo (Kanbo), showing where their father went on his trips to West Africa. Daughter Claire recalls how her mother used the map to explain how Felix's efforts at the plantation benefited the Noblia family chocolate business. Raymonde expanded the concept of the map to focus on where Basques lived throughout the world. She was meticulous about which names to include and used the Basque names for towns whenever possible.

In 1953, Raymonde gave eleven-year-old Claire the opportunity to begin her own quest for Basqueness. Together

they attended public classes in Basque culture held in the eve-
nings at the Biarritz (Miarritze) city hall. They continued this
activity for two years. The weekly sessions were taught by a
retired police officer, named Arburu, whose lively presentations about various Basque traditions kept Claire interested.
In 1954, Raymonde gave birth to her sixth child, Marianne,
and Claire began taking lessons in Euskara. The lessons were
private because at the time the French government did not
allow B>asque to be taught in school. Indeed, with the still
recent memory of a humiliating wartime experience fueling
a strong wave of French nationalism, interest in minority
cultures was widely viewed with suspicion and even hostility.
Consequently a nun instructed Claire for an hour a week for
two years.

Raymonde gave birth to her seventh child, Maialen,
in 1956. At this time, Claire committed herself to writing a
weekly letter in Euskara to her father. She persisted with these
weekly missives for over a year, until she passed her secondary
school exams in June of 1957 at the precocious age of fifteen.
After that, the letters were less frequent but still always in Euskara. Raymonde and Felix had habitually spoken French to
their children at home, but Claire would become so proficient
in the language that later she would decide to communicate
with her own children in Euskara.

Raymonde's Odyssey Continues

After the birth of Raymonde's eighth and last child, Véronique, she and Claire pursued their paths to Basqueness inde-
pendently. While Claire attended the University of Bordeaux,
Raymonde persisted in her genealogical research. In the early
1960s, her archival research led to her own genealogical gold-
en fleece when she found proof of her own Basque heritage.
Through the lineage of her maternal grandmother, Ida Mou-
lia, she traced a number of Basque ancestors. First, she found

a great-great-grandmother in the fourth ascendant generation, plus that same woman's father. Then another lineage
proved to have a Basque great-great-great-grandmother. In
a third lineage, Raymonde was able to document five ancestral Basque lines that included three great-great-great-great-
grandmothers and two great-great-great-great-grandfathers.
When she reached the seventh ascendant generation in the
early 1700s, Raymonde traced five additional lines. In all, she
uncovered ten Basque lineages with the following names: Ar-
mendariz, Darmendarry, Dastugue, Duhart, Labat, Laborde,
Labourdete, Lissague, Malgorry and Poylo/Pouillo.

In the late 1960s, as her youngest child Véronique turned
ten, Raymonde went to work in a long-established religious
bookstore called *La Porche* (the porch), close to the Bayonne
cathedral. Soon after, she bought the business but then discovered in 1970 that she would be evicted as the city had decided
to demolish the entire building. Raymonde had to relocate.
This gave her the opportunity to rent a place large enough to
add a whole new category of books by and about the Basques.
She reopened her business under the name "Jakin" because in
Basque it means "to know, to become informed, to discover."

By the end of the 1970s, Raymonde was ready to slow
down. She turned over many of the responsibilities at the
bookstore to her third child, Agnès, who had been assisting
her for many years. This left Raymonde time to summarize
her thirty-seven years of genealogical research in the form
of a chart. It took considerable ingenuity to present both the
Noblia and Richard lineages with clarity because of the sheer
numbers of family forebears she had documented. In total
she found 113 ancestors, reaching back to the late 1600s. The
chart had to show both Felix Noblia's thirty-eight ancestors
and her own seventy-five progenitors, including the forty-
seven Basques she had documented in the lineage of her maternal grandmother.

Claire's Odyssey

Raymonde's daughter Claire, following the family tradition, began studying medicine in 1958. During this period she also joined a Basque cultural association to take part in various activities and to practice her Euskara. Through this association, she met Lazaro Arandia-Iraz Usta, a Spanish Basque pelota player who spoke little French, and they were married in 1965, just as she finished her medical school course work.

Like her mother before her, Claire had ample opportunity to demonstrate the traditional Basque character traits of *indarra* and *sendotasuna*. Within twenty-four months, she wrote and presented a thesis on the role of hormonal factors in mastitis while serving five of her required hospital residencies. She also gave birth to her first child, a son named Aitor, in 1966. Because her husband was often unemployed, she accepted hospital assignments whenever possible during 1967 in order to earn money, even while fulfilling the requirements for the special certificate in anesthesiology. During all of this, she was pregnant with her second son, Mikel, who was born that year. When she went to Paris in September for the required written exam, she took two-week-old Mikel with her. She passed that exam and graduated with a special certificate in anesthesiology from the University of Bordeaux.

Claire worked full-time with two small children. Her third son, Ellande, was born early in 1969, and Claire continued to work after his arrival. During this time, she became involved in yet another Basque activity, this one both practical and ideological. Inspired by the clandestine Euskara-only *ikastola* educational movement among Basques in Spain, Claire decided to start a school of her own. An ikastola is a school in which all the subjects are taught in Euskara. The movement arose among Spanish Basques committed to preserving their unique language in the face of Spanish dictator Francisco Franco's formidable repression. Claire hired a young Basque-speaking woman, a trained teacher, to preside over the ikas-tola she formed for her two older sons and the offspring of friends. Classes were held in Claire's apartment. When the noise of the children began to bother the landlord who lived downstairs, however, she rented quarters big enough to allow for the inclusion of more children in the classes. At this point, she encouraged the parents to form an association, suggesting the word *Seaska* (cradle) for its name. The following year the association hired two more teachers and started two more nursery classes in Bayonne and St. Jean de Luz (Donibane-Lohizune).

Claire served as the president of Seaska for six years. During that time, she managed to travel to the Ivory Coast in 1972 to visit her father, Felix, on the plantation. She also had two more sons, Odon in 1974 and Ortzi in 1976. Meanwhile, Seaska expanded geographically to include eight locations. Its facility in Bayonne increased to five class levels, two of them preschool and three at the primary levels. By May of 1999, Seaska was operating twenty-two schools and serving 1,732 students, including more than 300 at the secondary school level. That same year one hundred thousand people celebrated Seaska's thirtieth anniversary.

By 1976, Claire was working full time, raising five children, and running Seaska. But that was not enough. She also initiated a statistical analysis of the incidence of Basque suicide reported in twenty years of hospital records from Iparralde. She discovered that many more Basque women than men attempted suicide, but more Basque men than women actually succeeded in killing themselves. The resulting thesis earned her an additional degree from the University of Bordeaux in 1978.

In 1982, Claire passed a national exam in Paris that qualified her as a consulting physician for the medical service of the French national social security system. Her first assignment was in Mont de Marsan, fifty miles away from home. For four years, she commuted during the week, leaving after dinner on Monday and returning Friday evening. During her absence, her two youngest sons stayed with a nearby orthodontist friend while her three oldest slept at Loreduna where her mother, Raymonde, still lived.

When her father, Felix, died at the Sankadiokrou plantation in 1984, Claire traveled to the Ivory Coast to arrange for his funeral and burial on his beloved plantation. Claire was now the family member responsible for the plantation, and would return every year to spend a month there, overseeing the operation first hand, until it was sold in 1997. During her visits there, she also honored her father's dedication to the dispensary by taking medicines with her to replenish its inventory and by treating the sick that came to its door.

Claire subsequently reestablished her anesthesiology office in Bayonne in 1986. She also supervised her mother's care at Loreduna until Raymonde's death, at the age of 71, in 1987. In 1989, Claire again demonstrated her interest in local issues by accepting the invitation of Henri Grenet, the mayor of Bayonne and her former surgery professor, to affiliate herself with his list of candidates standing for election to the city council. She was elected, and she served on the city council until 1995. During this time she was a vocal and contentious watchdog for Basque concerns, and achieved one of her most important goals in 1990 when she convinced the mayor to provide an appropriate rent-free space for the local Seaska nursery and primary school. This large space accommodated the inclusion of secondary-level students, aged eleven to fourteen. Her success would subsequently influence the city council's decision in 1999 to provide even more space in order to incorporate students aged fifteen to eighteen.

In 1996 Claire was invited, as the founder of Seaska, to be one of two representatives from Iparralde to participate in a

Christmas program filmed that year by Euskal Telebista, the Basque television network in the Spanish Basque Country. Accompanied by the popular music group Oskorri, from Hegoalde or the southern side of the Basque Country, she presented several short songs in Euskara.

A year later, as her sons were grown, Claire decided to close her office and sell her house in Bayonne. She then moved to "Uhagun," a rural house she inherited from her father. Felix had purchased Uhagun because it had a mill that he used for processing cacao beans. Claire began clearing away debris that had accumulated on the property and in the process found a copy of a map that dated back to 1454. The map showed both a mill and a house exactly at the location of Uhagun. Fortunately for Claire, the original house had been substantially rebuilt in 1750, and during the 1920s electricity had been installed. After moving to Uhagun, Claire began accepting writing assignments on various subjects dealing with Basques. For one such project, she prepared the preface for Eric Chauche's volume of photographs of Iparralde, *Euskadi: Pays des Basques,* published in 1998. She was recommended for the task by Pierre Oyhamburu, a family friend who had been Raymonde's Euskara teacher fifty years before.

In the spirit of rediscovering her Basqueness, Claire began making improvements on the water-powered mill on her property with the goal of eventual restoration as an educational center. To aid in these efforts she has toured mills in other countries, including a 150-year-old grist mill in northern California which she visited in the' company of the author in 1999. She took numerous photographs of that mill and the historical displays associated with it, and applied what she learned to the restoration of her own mill and her house at Uhagun.

Claire's interest in the politics of Labourd (Lapurdi), the Basque province in Iparralde where she grew up, continued as she supported the political publication *La Feuille* (the paper) and attended the inauguration in 2000 of a *club-galerie* in Bayonne, sponsored by *La Feuille*. She also grew more interested in supporting the candidacy of young people with ardent Basque political views.

Conclusion

In the tradition of early Basque explorers, Raymonde and Claire Noblia's lives were voyages of discovery toward reclaiming their Basqueness. Their journey took them to the cultural heart of their homeland. Their story suggests that an on-going process of self-identification can make one more fully Basque. It can also influence those whose lives they touch.

Since meeting Claire Noblia in 1987, the author has received a great deal of information about Basque culture and used this in many articles. She spoke with me in 1996 about Raymonde's life and the genealogical chart, which she loaned to me for analysis. In 1998, I made my first visit to Uhagun, and Claire showed me Raymonde's small calendar from 1940. We also perused her mother's photos, including some from her days as a medical student in Paris, some from the Ivory Coast plantation, and others from her trek across the Sahara. In a return visit to my home in 1999, Claire visited two sessions of my class for adults, "Euskaldunak Everywhere" (Basques Everywhere), to sing Basque songs and answer a variety of questions for my students. In addition, she has been invaluable as a source of information for this article, providing facts and details about the journeys she and her mother took to become Basque.

Being of Basque blood does not automatically instill any knowledge of the language or interest in the culture, past or present. Raymonde and Claire Noblia have demonstrated that a desire to focus on Basqueness is much more instrumental in generating the interest and vitality necessary for transmitting an ancient patrimony to future generations. Their lives should encourage those who have only recently discovered their Basque heritage, and their *euskarapen* or "becoming Basque" should inspire those who have not yet made the journey toward their own.

Claire said, "Tell our story." I have tried to do that. And she added, "You are never too old to embark on becoming Basque."

Monique Laxalt:
A Literary Interpreter for
the New Generations of
Basque-Americans
David Río

In 1977 Richard W Etulain, one of the most distinguished
scholars of western American literature, published a brilliant
article analyzing the major literary treatments of American
Basques. He concluded his article with a series of general observations about the traditional role of the Basques in these
writings:

> Too many fictional works have dealt only with the
> Basque as a herder. [...] Because authors of belletristic
> writing have concentrated on the herder, they have
> tended to omit the experiences of Basque women and
> urbanites and the affairs of the second and third gen-
> eration. Too little has been written about problems
> of assimilation and Americanization. [56]

a_____

The research for this article was carried out within the framework of
the projects UPV 103.130-HA068/98, UPV 103.130-HA090/99, and
1/UPV 00103.130-H-13999/2001.

56   Richard W Etulain, "The Basques in Western North American Literature," in *Anglo-American Contributions to Basque Studies: Essays in Honor
of Jon Bilbao,* eds. William A. Douglass, Richard W. Etulain and William
H. Jacobsen, Jr. (Reno: Desert Research Institute Publications on the
Social Sciences, no. 13, 1977), p. 16.

Together with these references to the typical weaknesses and limitations of fictional Basque portraits, Etulain pointedly added that, "no American Basque, except Robert Laxalt, has written significant imaginative literature about his ethnic heritage." [57]

Sixteen years later Monique Laxalt, Robert Laxalt's daughter, published *The Deep Blue Memory* (as Monique Urza), a novel that may be viewed as the perfect response to the challenge posed by Etulain in his article. First of all, this book heralded a shift in perspective from the first-generation Basque sheepherder to his descendants in America. This shift, which had already been anticipated by ELobert Laxalt's *The Basque Hotel* (1989), displays exceptional features such as the writer's emphasis on younger Basque-Americans (particularly on the third generation, the grandchildren of immigrants) and her use of a female perspective to portray the conflict between loyalty to one's ethnic heritage and Americanization. Furthermore, publication of *The Deep Blue Memory* was significant in that it provided the Basque-American community with a new voice to describe and explain their experiences in the New World. Monique Laxalt's novel also served as an ideal companion to her father's books through its ability to portray a similar world from a different point of view. Indeed, as William A. Douglass has noted,

> read in tandem, father's and daughter's works, in addition to providing a satisfying literary experience of the highest order, provide the reader with a social commentary on "becoming American" that is quite unique within the literature on the nation's immigrant heritage. [58]

---

57   Ibid.

58   William A. Douglass, "Three for the Show," *The Basque Studies Newsletter*, vol. 48 (1993), p. 6.

Monique Laxalt, granddaughter of Basque immigrants to Nevada, was born in Reno in 1953. Her childhood in this city is brilliantly described in her first published story, "Sin City Children" (1976), an insightful approach to her peculiar memories of growing up in Reno. As Laxalt herself recalls in this story,

> a child can spend his growing-up years in a town such as Reno, Nevada, remembering more than anything else, not the lights of Virginia Street or the slot machines at the grocery store...but the summers and winters, and the smells of dust and sagebrush, autumn and new grass. [59]

Being the daughter of Robert Laxalt, unanimously acknowledged as the main literary spokesman for the Basque-Americans since the success of his masterful tale of immigration in *Sweet Promised Land* (1957), imbued Monique Laxalt with a strong Basque identity from her early childhood. Indeed, from an early age she was more conscious of a Basque identity than her father because as a child of Old World immigrants, he was forced to integrate more abruptly into American society, whereas by the time he was an adult and parent, he was looking back to his roots with an air of nostalgia. Although Monique Laxalt had an Anglo-Saxon heritage through her mother, the influence of her father's family was somehow more dominant and, together with her brother and sister, she considered herself primarily Basque. [60]

Monique's Basque identity was strongly reinforced in these early years through the umerous visits that she and her family made to the Basque Country. She was seven when she

---

59 Monique Laxalt, "Sin City Children," *Nevada Magazine*, vol. XXX-VI, no. 3 (1976), p. 21.

60 See David Río, "The Miraculous Blend: An Interview with Monique Urza," *Journal of the Society of Basque Studies in America*, vol. XVI (1996), p. 1.

first went ton the land of her forefathers in September 1960. The Laxalts took a yearlong sabbatical to live in Euskal Herria, spending half the year in Saint-Jean-de-Luz/Donibane Lohitzune and the remaining half in Saint-Jean-Pied-de-Port/Donibane Garazi. Monique remembers this time as a difficult and overwhelming one, mainly due to the ordeals that she had to face at school. She was placed in schools where all the subjects were taught in French, a language she was not familiar with, for eight or nine hours a day. Moreover, she had to endure a lot of teasing from her schoolmates due to the presence of a certain anti-American sentiment at the time. As a result, she never felt like an insider in the Basque Country. Curiously however, when she and her family returned to the United States, she started to feel like an outsider in her own country. Reintegrating back into America became a real adjustment for her. It is no wonder, then, that she has referred to her first trip to the Basque Country as "an intense experience with a lot of contradictions." [61]

Monique and her family went to live in Euskal Herria a second time at the end of 1965. After initially residing in Arcachon, at Christmas they decided to move once more to Donibane Garazi, where they spent about half a year. This time the adjustment to Basque life was easier for Monique because she already .knew the place, the people and their customs, as well as being a little older and wiser herself. [62] Although the fact that she was a foreigner still implied some hard experiences there, all in all it was a rewarding period for Monique, a time of discovery and productivity in which she learnt more about her heritage. Subsequently she would return to the Basque Country when she was twenty, under a university program, and on later occasions with her husband (in 1976 she married Carmelo Urza, another descendant of Basque immigrants to the United States) and her two children. However, it seems

---

61   Ibid., p. 2.

62   Ibid.

that Monique's most significant memories of the Basque Country come from her first two trips there, as evinced, for example, in the second chapter of *The Deep Blue Memory,* a section called "The Citadel," which is largely drawn from Monique's own experiences as a child growing up in Donibane Garazi.

Monique's childhood and early youth were not only marked by an awareness of her Basque identity, but also by the influence of her father's writing career. As she herself has stated, within her family writing and literature in general were regarded as fundamental values. [63] Consequently, after finishing high school in Reno it came as no surprise that she chose to pursue a university career related to literature. She received her first university degree (a B.A. in English) at Stanford. She then moved to the University of Iowa where she earned a master's degree in French Literature, completing a further year's study in Comparative Literature. However, she eventually decided to study law, receiving a Doctorate in Jurisprudence from the University of Iowa. Thereafter she became a member of the Nevada Bar in 1982, specializing in civil practice with an emphasis on legal writing. She described the interaction between law and literature in her life in the following way:

> I think that you can find the basis for art or writing in any profession. I don't think that art or whatever is such a separate thing... I do at times straight analytical writing and brief writing for the court. I'm so used to this fairly rigid writing that at first I thought I'd never be able to write anything else. But I think the whole experience helped me tremendously because it gave me discipline in terms of focusing in, and also in terms of trying to communicate to someone else. [64]

63   Ibid, p. 3.

64   Ibid., p.13.

Laxalt's interest in creative writing was present from an early age. She wrote different pieces, particularly poems, which she regarded mainly as a private experience, as "a way to stay in touch with some kind of beauty." [65] In 1981 she published "Catherine Etchart: A Montana Love Story," a non-fiction narration dealing with the life of a Basque immigrant woman in America. It is a story that, due to both its content and style might plausibly be considered as the inspiration, at least to a certain extent, for *The Deep Blue Memory*. In Monique's own words,

> there is some link between them, though not really conscious. Particularly I remember that when I was working on the story about Catherine Etchart I had an odd feeling because when I went up to Montana and stayed with her family, I felt like I should be writing about my own family. I think it was a really good experience for me, too, because I could take more objectivity. Anyway, I enjoyed it a lot and the story made me think a lot about my own family, too. Certainly there were some similarities and differences between the two families. [66]

It was not until 1990 that Monique decided to take a couple of years off from law practice in order to start writing *The Deep Blue Memory*. In her decision to become a writer she was obviously influenced by her father's literary devotion. Indeed she viewed her own writing as a validation of his career, as a way to express admiration for the life her father had chosen. At the same time she was conscious of the fact that being the daughter of a distinguished author conditioned somehow her own sense of reality and, in particular, her potential writ-

65 Ibid., p.12.

66 Ibid., pp. 4-5.

ing. As Monique recalls, "so many experiences were reflected through my father's writing that... I was feeling as if I should write about certain things, like the Basque Country, as he saw them."[67]

The Deep Blue Memory can be interpreted as the result of Monique's need to explore her own identity and, in particular, the twin condition of an American upbringing laced with a Basque heritage. The novel emphasizes the importance of every process of exploration, as symbolized by her choice of T. S. Eliot's quotation as the epigraph of the book.[68] Laxalt herself has referred to the writing of the novel as a personal learning process:

> When I sat down to write the book I just knew I had to try to put something down on paper and give a form to certain things I had experienced. Then at a certain point of the writing process I did realize that I was trying to figure out the basic identity complex between the Basque heritage and the American identity, and between the different role models (grandparents, parents...), and also the sense of family versus individuality. So, the quote from T. S. Eliot seemed specially fitting because that was exactly what I discovered.[69]

The novel can also be interpreted as an attempt to understand the role of the ethnic legacy in contemporary American society. The author herself has acknowledged that the book was prompted by an interest in exploring the meaning

---

67   Ibid., pp. 3-4.

68   "We shall not cease from exploration/And the end of our exploring/Will be to arrive where we started/And know the place for the first time." T.S. Eliot, "Little Gidding," quoted in the epigraph of Monique Laxalt (as Monique Urza), *The Deep Blue Memory* (Reno: University of Nevada Press, 1993).

69   Río, "The Miraculous Blend," p. 5.

of a Basque heritage for her children's generation. [70] While usually aware and proud of their roots, younger Basque-Americans do not feel such a frantic need to research their ethnic identity, as was often the case with earlier generations. A Basque heritage is not as psychologically central to these descendants of immigrants, concerned with developing their own individuality in a multicultural society where most of them feel at home. As Laxalt herself remarks,

> I was aware that here through immigration, and this is something that I especially started feeling when I had children, we are becoming further and further away from any kind of continuity and tradition, and our children after us. And it was a very confusing feeling because I identified a lot with the Basque people and yet in a lot of ways I was thinking I cannot be more different from them than anyone else on earth. I guess that in the book a lot of that came up: the vast individuality and the recognizing that your kids are just people. They don't need those things (the "caserio", the land...) and you don't need them, either, because a person is an individual. [71]

The Deep Blue Memory draws upon the experiences of the writer's own family to describe the way in which different generations of a Basque family in Nevada come to terms with the immigration experience. The narrator of the story never reveals the surname of the family, but its identity is not completely disguised. In fact, any reader familiar with the story of the Laxalts would notice a number of similarities between the main characters in the novel and different members of this prominent Basque-American family. For example, the narrator's immigrant grandparents are markedly similar to Monique's own, as is her father (Anthony, a brilliant writ-

---

70   Ibid., p. 7.

71   Ibid., p. 9.

er) to Robert Laxalt. Similarly one of the characters, Uncle Luke, closely resembles Paul Laxalt (Robert's brother), who became Nevada governor, served two terms in the U.S. Senate and was considered as a candidate for the presidency in 1988. And, of course, there is common ground between the narrator and Monique Laxalt herself. However, *The Deep Blue Memory* remains a novel, a work written as a piece of fiction, as emphasized at its very beginning. In fact, Monique has always insisted on this idea when asked about the importance of autobiographical elements in her novel:

> I didn't want the book to be like a biography of the Laxalt family or something like that. And in the editorial process I had to stand up for myself on that point... I didn't use the Laxalt name at all in the book, even in my name. Definitely an important part of the book is autobiographical. However, I did fictionalize certain things... I would describe the book as psychologically autobiographic. People have a need, an inherent human need to take their own life and express it in some concrete way. [72]

In *The Deep Blue Memory* Laxalt portrays the complexity of the immigration process through different generations of the same family. Within this portrayal she resorts to the juxtaposition of a series of images to underscore the clash between modern American ways and older Basque values. This clash is further exposed through the conflict between the rewards brought by assimilation into American society and the price to be paid for integration and success. It is a conflict that each generation has to deal with on its own terms.

The first generation of immigrants is represented in the book by the narrator's Basque grandparents, who settled as sheep ranchers in Nevada. They are reluctant to lose their

---

72   Ibid., pp. 5-6.

ethnic identity in exchange for integration and acceptance, though they are aware that their descendants may have to follow a different path. This generational gap is illustrated in the book by the attitude of their five children, the second generation. They are immigrant siblings who will work hard to overcome prejudice and achieve professional success and recognition in the United States. Their acceptance of American standards does not imply a rejection of their heritage per se, but this will inevitably be affected by the overwhelming impact of the process of Americanization at the level of the second generation. As a consequence, their children, the nineteen cousins mentioned in the book, will be subject to contradictory influences illustrated by different images of both the New and Old Worlds. Furthermore, generational differences are highlighted once more because these grandchildren of immigrants do not feel the same pressure as their forebears to be successful. In fact, the American Dream has already become a reality for the whole family through their parents' efforts. As such, the third generation, in spite of their full integration into American society, looks back to its roots, to an invaluable heritage that it is afraid of losing through Americanization. In this sense, members of the third generation feel closer to their grandparents than to their parents. Finally, the fourth generation, represented in the book by the narrator's own children, seems to symbolize the accomplishment of the immigration process. The past is no longer so important for them as they feel completely at home in America. These great-grandchildren of immigrants may be proud of their heritage but they do not feel its presence as a psychologically central factor in developing their own sense of reality. As the narrator observes at the end of the book, they do "not need the view down on the deep blue jewel and the pale blue expanse beyond it to see clearly." [73]

---

73   Laxalt (as Urza), *The Deep Blue Memory*, p. 156.

In *The Deep Blue Memory* Laxalt demonstrates the achievement of the narrator's family in America through the brilliant careers of the five children of the immigrant Basque sheep ranchers. Although all five brothers manage to obtain important rewards in their professional lives, it is Uncle Luke who best embodies the success story of this Basque family. His meteoric political career, first as Nevada governor and later in the U.S. Senate, represents the rise to power of the descendants of immigrants, of the second generation bent on achieving their own American Dream. Through Uncle Luke's success, the narrator's family rises from obscurity and immigrant prejudice to become arguably the most prominent family in Nevada. Even the narrator's grandmother, a character who seems to remain absolutely detached from the intrigues of the political world, obtains recognition, being chosen Mother of the Year in Nevada. The rewards, then, of personal achievement for the whole family are obvious yet the novel also implies that the price to be paid for this success is ultimately too high: in effect, the violation of the treasured privacy of a Basque family.

In Laxalt's book the reader is offered a brilliant description of the transformation, produced by political success, of the narrator's family: in many ways they relinquish their status as private citizens to become public property. Through Uncle Luke's visibility the whole family becomes a sitting target for the public, as both the aspiring politician and his relatives have to face a common ordeal: namely, personal attacks in the mass media from rival candidates as alluded to in the book by "the allegation that was black in color." [74] As a result, the harsh nature of politics not only invades family privacy, but also brings into question its respectability. In fact, Uncle Luke's rise to power might be interpreted as an initiation process for the whole family, whose name becomes synonymous with the ballot box.

---

74   Ibid., p. 92.

The story of this Basque family in Nevada raises yet a further bittersweet observation of the consequences of the immigrant success: the sacrifice of a genuine identity. This sacrifice is directly connected in the book with Uncle Luke's rise to power, which provokes the need to explain in public a series of private symbols, often linked to the family's own heritage and background. Thus the family name, its immigrant story and its Basque traditions become public property. Yet this increasingly becomes not just a matter of vanishing privacy, but also of increasing artificiality, particularly notorious when these symbols are politically marketed. *The Deep Blue Memory* alludes to this through the work written by the narrator's father, "the deep blue book" [75] dealing with the story of her grandfather and her family heritage, which will be used to help Uncle Luke to win a seat in the U.S. Senate. We can sense, then, that the genuine characteristics of the narrator's family are gradually subordinated to success in, and recognition by, American society, becoming more and more artificial as the public notoriety increases. Ultimately, the new prominence of the family imposes on its members a commitment to a specific identity that is no longer a private matter, but a question of public image.

At another, though related, level, *The Deep Blue Memory* can also be analyzed as a masterful account of the tensions between loyalty to the family group and the individual's natural process of searching for his/her own identity. The tale thus becomes a conflict between concern for the family group and its heritage and the desire to develop one's own personality, a subject that also plays a pivotal role in Robert Laxalt's Basque-family trilogy: *The Basque Hotel* (1989), *Child of the Holy Ghost* (1992) and *The Governor's Mansion* (1994). To borrow terminology developed by Werner Sollors (in *Beyond Ethnicity*. New York: Oxford University Press, 1986), Monique Laxalt's

---

75   Ibid., p. 14 *et al.*

novel thus reveals an exploration of the tensions between "descent" and "consent" relations, between ancestral or hereditary bonds and self-made or contractual identity.

The book ultimately evokes the power of family bonds among the Basques and emphasizes the unity of the narrator's family as the key factor to understand its success in America. "The creature called family"[76] is portrayed as a closely-knit unit, whose survival is entrusted to each of its members. It is a sacred circle, "a fortress," to use the narrator's own words,[77] where each individual contributes to the betterment of the group as a whole. In fact, family devotion emerges as a fundamental element for immigrants bound together in overcoming prejudice and achieving success in America. The immigrant family remains intact principally out of necessity, and this unity turns out to be essential when the family has to face the negative dimensions and turmoil of the political world. Thus Uncle Luke represents the underdog who has to fight against more powerful rivals, "against money and connections that went three generations back."[78] Furthermore, his campaigns are family efforts where individual members subdue their personal views and aims in order to contribute to a common goal: his, and therefore a familial, political success. It is a self-imposed discipline of duty to the family group which cannot be conceived as a temporary effort, but rather as a permanent commitment because success may also bring several risks for the family: internal divisions and outside attacks. Indeed, as the narrator remembers, "the *stronger* the family, the more valuable it is, the more *vulnerable* it is, the more needful of protection."[79]

---

76   Ibid., p. 27 *et al.*

77   Ibid., p. 67.

78   Ibid., p. 65.

79   Ibid., p. 113.

The Deep Blue Memory celebrates the power and rewards of family solidarity while demonstrating the hindrance that this obligation implies to the personal development of its different members. The book portrays the family as a fundamental source of strength for the descendants of immigrants, but it also underscores the importance of consent-based relations for their proper development as individuals. As a result, the traditional unity of the Basque family has to compete in the novel with the typical American devotion to individuality.

In particular, the book highlights the potential damage of overemphasizing family obligations through its examination of descent relations. When too many experiences are reflected through the family, when its individual members breathe as one, they run the risk of losing their own personal identity. This idea is closely linked in the novel to the increasing success and public notoriety of the narrator's family. The different kin have to sacrifice a part of their individuality to contribute to the common well being of the family. The price turns out to be particularly high when faced with a serious allegation made against the family, first by a political opponent and later by a rival newspaper. The tragic end of this episode, symbolized by Aunt Sondra's suicide, illustrates the risks of commitment to a family that undervalues individual feelings. When respectability, as represented by a prominent and glowing family name, is given priority over the family itself, its individual members may lose their own sense of reality and even their emotional stability. Therefore, loyalty to the family group and devotion to its heritage should not become an obstacle for the individual's natural desire to choose his/her own destiny. One's search for identity should be always based on personal freedom, as symbolized at the end of the book by the narrator's new awareness of her son's face:

> I looked at the young face and suddenly I knew that
> I had never looked at it before, the face that bore
> nothing of the dark earth, the face that was as open,
> as unrestrained, as free as these desert hills. [80]

The Deep Blue Memory portrays the process of exploration of one's ethnic identity as a never-ending experience: as progress towards the future while at the same time remaining sensitive to remembering and understanding the past. It would, therefore, come as no surprise if in future works Monique Laxalt returned to the theme of contemporary Basque-American identity. In fact, at present she is writing a novel that deals in part with the Basque heritage, although as one of the many such legacies in the United States. Indeed her future seems most promising because above all, she is, as her father defined her in a 1996 interview, [81] an honest writer.

---

80   Ibid., p. 156.

81   See David Río, "A Basque Voice in the Promised Land: An Interview with Robert Laxalt," *Revista Española de Estudios Norteamericanos,* vol. 12 (1996), p. 130.

Interconnected Disconnectedness: How Diaspora Basque Women Maintain Ethnic Identity

Gloria Pilar Totoricagüena

We left the Basque country for political reasons. One of our daughters is in prison as a convicted ETA sympathizer, and another daughter decided to stay in Donostia, so we go home often. Brussels is close and it is easy to keep up with the events in Euskadi. We will go back some day after she is released. I will not live in a country where my daughter is in a cage (Egibar, Belgium 1997).

I don't ever remember a time when I didn't know I was Basque. Although my parents didn't speak to me in Basque, my mother spoke to her mother in Basque. My grandparents came to the U.S. from Ibarrengelua and wanted to forget the old country. They couldn't. I was born in the U.S. and thought I could be like the Americans. I can't (Lejardi, United States 1997).

The Catholic Church paid my way. I came to Sydney with a group of thirty single Basque women, chaperoned by one Priest, looking for adventure and possibly a mate. They expected us to stay at least two years or we would have to reimburse them the costs.

> I married a Basque man here in Australia and so did most of the others. I love Australia and I love Euskal Herria; I don't have to be one or the other (Salazar, Australia 1996).

> Fifth generation Uruguayan. Can you imagine that I just visited my family's farmhouse near Donibane Garazi for the first time? I wept. I wept for all that I have missed. For that which my parents and grand-parents never knew. All of my ancestors in Uruguay died without knowing, without feeling, without smelling, without completing. Can you imagine that I have just visited my family's farmhouse (Maytia 1995).[82]

In November of 1995, Vitoria-Gasteiz, the capital city of the Autonomous Basque Community, hosted the First World Congress of Basque Collectivities. The fourteen different countries sending delegates were as diverse as Canada with a few thousand Basques and one formal organization in the making, to Argentina, which boasts of nearly ninety Basque organizations. Delegates had been elected or appointed by their organizations to travel to Euskal Herria, to help the Autonomous Basque Government formulate policy regarding Basques in the diaspora.

Curiously these Basques had more in common than not. Comments from interviews, such as those mentioned above, revealed very similar responses whether from fourth genera-

---

82   My qualitative and quantitative research data are based on 186 personal interviews and 818 anonymous questionnaires administered in the five countries between 1995 and 1998. All respondents are self-identifying Basques who participate in a Basque institution, or where no established Basque institution exists, have shown interest in collective action to promote Basque culture and identity. Stratified samples were used to assure representation by gender, generation, income, level of education, age, and Basque Center subgroups such as athletes, musicians, artists, dancers, language class students, choir members, chefs, mus players, elected Directors, and members not involved in any sub-groups. The personal interviews were primarily conducted in a person's home or at a Basque Center, and snowball samples ensured representativeness.

tion Uruguayans, fifth generation Argentineans, first generation Australians, or second generation Belgians: "we are Basques who live outside of the homeland but that does not make us any less Basque." Until this Congress, these people had not met each other, nor had any of these organizations ever interacted with each other with the exception of Argentina with Uruguay. According to generally accepted theories of acculturation and assimilation, these Basques should have all been very distinct from each other because of the influence of the host society to which their ancestors had emigrated. By the fifth generation, these theories argue, characteristics common of the new society should be exhibited. Why then was there so much homogeneity and consensus in their views toward ethnonationalism and ethnic identity maintenance when their host societies are so different from one another? In an attempt to answer these questions I will compare different emigration experiences, definitions of "Basqueness," and cultural preservations in these five countries.

Women in Migration

Women have been essentially omitted from early studies of migration and, when considered at all, have been perceived as amendments to the men who migrated; non-thinking, non-emotional appendages with no choices, comparable to the valuable things packed in traveling trunks. They have been treated more as migrants' wives, daughters, and mothers than as migrants themselves, relegating their roles in international migration as secondary. In some instances, however, such as the United States, female migrants outnumber male migrants. [83] Because women are intimately involved with men any changes in their status obviously affects their male companions, and vice versa. It is erroneous, therefore, to perceive women as non-working dependents.

---

83   Rita James Simon and Caroline B. Brettle, eds. *International Migration: The Female Experience* (Totowa, NJ: Rowan and Allanheld, 1986), p. 4.

Basque women who migrated to Argentina and Uruguay entered host societies where Basques were historically recognized and highly regarded with a positive social status. Those in the United States were usually categorized as Spanish or French, whereas in Australia Basques were and still are commonly mistaken for Italian. The shock of migration for many Basques heading for South America came not so much from exchanging one country for another, but rather from exchanging a "country" for a city culture. Those migrating to Montevideo, Buenos Aires, or Rosario settled in urban environments of hundreds of thousands, or in some cases millions, of residents — a significant shift from the agricultural and fishing cultures of small villages and farmsteads from where they set out. Whether in Melbourne or Montevideo, San Francisco or Sydney, women stated that the demands of city life, in addition to the geographical and cultural change, could be overwhelming and the transition from traditional to modern was, and is, neither simple nor straightforward and linear.

The costs of migration are both personal and emotional, and Basque women have suffered the stress that accompanies surviving in a transnational double world, a stress that forces migrants to adapt rapidly and frequently to considerable changes in habits and expectations.[84] They also experience a lack of belonging and acceptance in both their homeland and host country, which was often mentioned as especially frustrating. In Australia, they are "the Basque woman," yet when visiting in Euskal Herria they are "the Australian woman." "En el limbo" (in limbo) was a phrase repeated often in each country, usually by emigrants themselves, but also by the first generation born in the host country. These women did not feel completely connected to their homeland or host country,

---

84   Basch, Linda, Nina Glick Schiller, and Christina Szanton Blanc. 1994. *Nations Unbound: Transnational Projects, Postcolonial Predicaments, and Deterritorialized Nation-States.* Amsterdam: Gordon and Breach Science Publishers S.A., p. 242.

in other words to no one single territory or culture. Yet they do feel solidly connected to each other because of their shared experiences. The physical disconnectedness to Euskal Herria is thus replaced by an emotional and intellectual interconnect- edness with other Basque women. Emigrants understand each other's horrors of political exile, loss of family and friends, and fears of dealing with new cultures in their host countries. First and second generation-born women in the host coun- tries understand each other's upbringing and how they are different from host country non-Basque friends. From con- stantly spelling and explaining their surnames, to describing food preparation, to interpreting ETA activities, women of all ages in each of the five settings declared that they believe they have more in common with each other in different countries than they do with other women equivalent to them in their own host countries. This imagined connection is developed, therefore, through their Basque ethnicity and its experiences. A free journal, *Euskal Etxeak* (Basque Centers), distributed to Basques in the diaspora by the Autonomous Basque Govern- ment of Euskadi (Araba, Bizkaia, Gipuzkoa) was often used as an example in conversations when women compared them- selves to other Basques in different countries. "They celebrate San Ignacio and have dancers and choirs the same way we do. I found a story about a girlfriend from my hometown, and she is just like me except she ended up in the United States and I escaped to Belgium. I bet she has fried as many chorizos and tortillas as I have." [85]

Do women preserve Basque traditions more than men, and what exactly is the woman's role in the reproduction and development of ethnicity in her family? The expected role of women as reproducers of ethnic practices and traditions is of- ten related to women being perceived as the "cultural carri- ers" of that ethnic group. Women are perceived as the main

---

85   Feliza Urriz Larragan, interview by author, Brussels, 1997.

socializers of young children, the teachers who transfer cultural traditions to the next generation. In the case of the emigrant generation they are often less assimilated because they work in the home. They are consequently less assimilated linguistically and socially within the wider society. However, the research data of Basque diaspora communities demonstrate no difference between males and females in their attitudes towards mothers or fathers being more influential in preserving and maintaining Basque ethnic traditions. Asked to react to the statement, "Mothers have been more influential than fathers for teaching Basque culture to their children," a majority disagreed or had no opinion. Only 36% of males and 40% of females agreed with this statement. Usually, then, socialization from host country peers (school, physical surroundings, and the media, for example) combines with Basque ethnic socialization from home, the Basque Centers, and cultural events with other Basque families, encouraged by both mothers and fathers.

Because in family migration, married couples tend to move to where the husband has the greatest opportunity for employment, there often remains great difficulty in disassociating men's and women's individual motivations and aspirations for migration. [86] Once in the host country, men tend to work outside the home and learn the host country language, customs, and expectations; in other words, how to "move" within the new society. Often the Basque woman's experience has not been so positive, especially in the English speaking United States and Australia. Many women narrated emotions of tremendous loneliness, isolation, and depression. They experienced a lack of both self-esteem and sense of self-worth from the inability to express themselves. They had, in many ways, been robbed of their youth, of their own dreams and aspirations. Basque organizations, therefore, be-

---

86   See Sylvia Chant, ed. *Gender and Migration in Developing Countries* (London: Belhaven Press, 1992).

came tremendously significant as outlets for these women to communicate through their ethnicity. And this communication between *haizpak* (sisters) through ethnic identity provided both empowerment and recognition for it gave them a history, a collective feeling, support from an ethnic "family," and self-worth. Within this communicative structure the Basque Centers have served as havens not only for ethnic self-statement, but also in providing other models of host country integration while at the same time preserving Basque culture, the continuity of tradition, and a place of belonging and connectedness.

Definitions of Basqueness

What definitions of "Basqueness" do the women of the diaspora maintain? Do they maintain a mindset associated with more conservative and exclusive categories of race/ancestry, language, and religion, or are they more in tune with a contemporary homeland that accepts those who live and work in Euskal Herria, and who promote and extend Basque culture, as Basque? Religious affiliation is generally considered to be one of many key factors in cultivating ethnic group solidarity, and Catholicism has been a historically significant factor in defining Basque identity. From the data, it would appear that religion continues to occupy an important role in defining Basque identity within the diaspora populations with 71% of females and 69% of males agreeing that "continuing Catholic beliefs and traditions in our Basque families" is of "great" or "very great" importance. Unsurprisingly, the older the woman, the higher the percentage that believed Catholicism was of "great" or "very great" importance.

Table 1. Maintainig Catholocism is of "great" or "very great" Importance by Age Category.

18-30yrs.	31-45 yrs.	45-60 yrs.	61-75 yrs.	76-90 yrs.
36%	54%	62%	71%	76%

Combined results of 400 female responses from all five countries.

In the United States, where many interviewees mentioned experiencing discrimination against Catholics, 80% of the females responded that it is of "some," "great" or "very great" importance to maintain the beliefs and traditions. Basques in Belgium were the least likely to think that religion was important to their ethnic identity, with only 33% agreeing with the statement, whereas these levels rose to 54% of Uruguayans, 66% of Argentines, and 67% of Australians respectively. Religion, then, tends to be a more significant factor in Basque Center celebrations in the United States, where a Catholic mass is normally a part of the *Aberri Eguna* (National Day), numerous festivals, and NABO (North American Basque Organizations) conventions. Therefore as the majority of Basque celebrations are related to Catholicism, in the United States the religious link to ethnic identity is maintained. In the other countries of the diaspora, as in Euskal Herria, the practice of religion has declined and festivals are celebrated and Saints commemorated without significant fanfare for their religious aspects. Mass is usually attended by a minority, and remains only a small part of generally secular celebrations (of dance, art, film, food, and sports, for example) that last from two days to the week-long program of the annual Argentine National Basque Week.

When considering the factor of ancestry in defining Basque identity, again, American women were the most conservative, whereas those residing in Belgium regarded the issue of least importance in their responses. Responding to the statement, "A person must have Basque ancestors to be Basque," 97% of the women in the United States "agreed" or "strongly agreed," while 60% of those in Belgium did so. In each country, at least a majority agreed (Argentina 66%, Uruguay 70%, Australia 73%). Age categories showed a difference only in the youngest group of 18-30 year olds, which also agreed that the ancestry factor was important (by 62%), while the other categories responded by much higher percentages and agreed by between 80% — 92%. Regardless of age, when comparing generations of emigrants themselves, between 70% and 88% of emigrants through to the third generation born in the host country believed ancestry to be necessary to defining Basque identity, but only 35% of fourth generation women agreed. The most recent generation, then, seems to be moving closer to homeland definitions of Basqueness. This may be due to their increased contact (both physical and virtual) with Euskal Herria in comparison to their forebears.

In a 1995 survey conducted in all seven provinces by the Basque Autonomous Government Department of Culture, for example, people responded that the most important conditions necessary for a person to be considered Basque were "to have been born in the Basque Country" (59%), "to live and work in the Basque Country" (51%), "to speak *euskera*" (27%), and "to comprehend and defend Basque culture and folklore" (15%). Indeed, only 10% thought that "to have Basque surnames" was important in defining Basque identity. [87] The marked difference between diaspora and homeland population regarding surnames (and therefore ancestry) illustrates the homeland's move toward a more civic and inclusive definition of Basque ethnic identity, compared with the diaspora's more traditional approach to defining Basqueness.

---

87   See Xabier Aizpurua, *Fa Continuidad del Euskera* (Vitoria-Gasteiz: Gobierno Vasco, Departamento de Cultura, Servicio Central de Publicaciones del Gobierno Vasco, 1995).

In the questionnaire responses, 39% of females and 43% of males did however agree that, "persons permanently living in Euskal Herria should be accepted as Basques whether or not they were born there." Moreover, within the diaspora a surprising 84% of the females and 86% of males that had regarded ancestry as necessary in defining ethnic identity also supported the idea of "accepting as Basques, those people who feel and identify themselves as Basques."

Differences between the women by country ranged from 100% of Basques in Belgium agreeing with this acceptance, to 74% in the United States. Personal interviews detected a general reluctance to accept "outsiders" but several interviewees believed that, "if the Catalans do it in Catalunya, the Basques should, too." Once more, as with the responses regarding Catholicism, Basque women in Belgium demonstrated a more civic and less biological definition of Basqueness. They are, of course, more recent immigrants transmitting a more contemporary ideology from their homeland. Furthermore, because of the physical proximity, they are able to visit the Basque Country more easily, more economically, and more frequently.

Basque Language Knowledge and Transmission

As a factor of Basque ethnic identity within the diaspora populations, Euskera has lost much of its importance. In Euskal Herria itself, already by the mid-1800s various areas had lost Basque through an increasing state presence that both promoted and forced the use of Spanish or French. Later, during the Franco era (1939 – 75) the Basque language was outlawed as a means of communication. Consequently, many emigrants fleeing the Basque Country in search of political exile did not themselves speak Basque. As the table below demonstrates, though diaspora Basques are extremely proud of their unique and complex language, most do not consider it an important factor in their own ethnicity, or, indeed, in categorizing others as Basque. The following table represents questionnaire responses from males and females of all age categories in the five separate countries, and also records the percentages of those that do actually speak the language.

Table 2. "To be considered a Basque, a person should speak the Basque langauage."

	Agree or strongly agree	No opinion	Disagree or strongly disagree	% of Respondents who do speak Basque fluently or with some difficulty
Belgium	13%	4%	83%	42%
Uruguay	12%	6%	83%	2%
United States	15%	9%	76%	46%
Argentina	24%	8%	68%	16%
Australia	36%	13%	52%	56%
Female	18%	9%	73%	31%
Male	21%	8%	71%	32%
aged 18-30	19%	8%	73%	25%
aged 31-45	20%	6%	74%	26%
aged 46-60	20%	7%	72%	27%
aged 61-75	18%	12%	70%	38%
aged 76-90	16%	14%	69%	61%

Total from 818 respondents from all five countries.

Although traditional Basque nationalism historically stressed the importance of the Basque language, and the last influential wave of migration involved people raised with this ideology, Basques in these diaspora countries no longer consider the language issue of such great importance. Obviously, as so many of them do not speak Euskera they would not want to eliminate themselves from the category of being Basque.

Finally, according to the data, there are no significant differences between male and female abilities or attitudes.

According to table 2, then, 31% of the total female respondents are able to speak Basque "fluently" or "with some difficulty." Table 3 further highlights just how few Basque women of the diaspora are actually able to speak and utilize Euskera, as well as how many are illiterate in their ancestral language. Respondents were asked to describe their language abilities and usage of Basque using five separate categories. Regarding female respondents alone, table 3 measures language ability, speaking frequencies, and literacy in Basque, and combines the responses of those who have "no Basque language at all" with those who can speak, use, and read and write "only a few words or special phrases such as 'Happy Birthday', or 'Congratulations':"

Table 3. Basque Language Familiarity, Usage, and Literacy

	Uruguay	Argentina	United States	Belgium	Australia
"I know only a few words" or "none at all"	94%	64%	44%	40%	33%
"I only use Basque for special phrases" or "none at all"	83%	48%	30%	30%	24%
"I can write only a few wors in Basque" or "none at all"	98%	61%	62%	40%	52%

Total of 400 femal respondents from all five countries

Until the early 1990s, the interior population of Uruguay lacked any Basque organizations and had to rely on the two Basque Centers in Montevideo for collective cultural fulfillment. Without any new migration, the need for, and interest in, Euskera basically evaporated. Today there are recreational Basque language classes that meet sporadically, but few serious students. That said, there are Euskera programs at Basque Centers in Argentina, Uruguay, Australia, and the United States, as well as university language courses and *ikastolak* (Basque language schools) in both Argentina and the United States. Yet while students and parents are to be commended for their tremendous efforts, sociolinguistic studies demonstrate that without a strong social or economic reason for learning and using a language, it is not likely to be maintained. Diaspora Basques can thus use Euskera with each other (if they are both one of the few who know it) but they can equally utilize their host country language without feeling any less Basque. When traveling or communicating with relatives in Euskal Herria, for example, those from Argentina and Uruguay can easily use Spanish, and those from Belgium would use French. However, Australian and United States Basques must learn a second language to communicate with other Basques in the homeland or in the diaspora, and they tend to take school courses in French or Spanish to become literate in one of their parents' languages. Interviewees often mentioned the academic and economic benefits of learning Spanish or French for future employment, while those in Argentina, Uruguay, and Belgium were inevitably studying English. Interestingly, in Euskal Herria non-Basque nationalists make the same argument for learning English rather than Basque. Unfortunately, French-speaking Basques from Belgium and Spanish-speaking Basques from Uruguay are utilizing English rather than Basque to communicate.

Political Behavior and Attitudes

For many in the diaspora, "Basqueness" carries with it a politi-
cal dimension that is, on the whole, private and not a salient
part of institutional practices such as Basque Center activities.
There are currently 32,858 people in the diaspora that retain
Spanish citizenship and therefore voting rights in the Basque
Autonomous Community (Araba, Bizkaia, Gipuzkoa) and a
further 12,690 Nafarroans abroad with the same rights in the
Foral Community of Nafarroa, although the figures are not
available for Iparralde (Lapurdi, Baxe Nafarroa, Zuberoa).[88]
Only a minority, however, of these people have actually reg-
istered to vote with the Basque Autonomous Community's
Government.

Table 4. 1999 Total Number per Country of Diaspora Registerd
Voters in the Basque Autonomous Community

Argentina	United States	Uruguay	Belgium	Australia
3,699	2,010	1,022	977	not available

Figures from Iñaki Aguirre, Basque Autonomous Community General
Secretary of Forein Action.

In the following poll, respondents were given nine
Basque political parties to choose from, as well as an "other"
option, yet in every country the traditional and conservative
Partido Nacionalista Vasco (PNV Basque Nationalist Party)
emerged as the most popular choice among the diaspora,
while the leftist, radical nationalist Herri Batasuna (HB

88 Iñaki Aguirre, Basque Autonomous Government Department of
Relations with the Diaspora, interview by author, March 2, 1999.

United Homeland/People's Unity, now renamed Batasuna)
came in second. More telling than the choice of party was
the respondent's willingness to select "I don't know enough
about Basque Country politics to answer this question,"
or "I purposefully stay out of Basque Country politics."
There were no significant differences between the genders
and there was little difference between age categories with
stronger support from the elderly for the PNV. Regardless
of age, 36% of the emigrant generation of females supported
the PNV, falling to only 5% of second-generation women.
In each category of gender, generation, or geography, the
majority did not participate in homeland politics, with the
exception of Basque women in Belgium who emerged as 78%
supportive of the PNV and 22% of HB. The proximity of
Belgium, the accessibility to news from the home country in
the daily media, and a more recent migration translating to
closer familial ties, increases Belgian Basques' interest and
participation in politics.

Table 5. "Which political party most closely fits your views in
the Basque Autonomous Community?"

	PNV	HB	I don't know enough about B.A.C. polictics to choose a party	I stay out of B.A.C. politics
Female	11%	5%	61%	18%
Male	20%	6%	52%	16%

Combined 818 responses from all five countries.

Diaspora Basques tend to prefer cultural rather than political activities and most of the Centers' statutes declare in writing that they are apolitical institutions. When comparing genders, 79% of males and 82% of females agreed with the statement that they "prefer to participate in Basque cultural events and not political events." Differences between generations were very small, with between 76% and 84% also preferring cultural events. Geographically, Belgium's Basques once again stood out with only a 58% agreement, while the Basques of the other countries agreed by an 80% margin. This is best explained by the fact that Brussels is home to the European Union's various branches of administrative government and Basques there have taken advantage of their freedom of expression in attempting to influence European Union policy toward civil rights for Basques in Spain. Belgian Basques are also much more likely than their diaspora kin to participate in political movements which have taken place in their host country if the movement directly affects Basques.

Table 6. "While living in (host country) have you ever participated in any political movements (rallies, letter-writing, protests, fund-raisers, etc.) specifically because it would affect Basques?"

	Argentina	Australia	Belgium	United States	Uruguay
No, because there have not been political movements that would affect Basques.	40%	52%	30%	41%	17%
No, because I do not get involved in politics.	54%	45%	26%	51%	75%
Total percentages of "not participating"	94%	97%	56%	92%	92%

What are the personal decisions and motivations involved in international migration? For many, one's homeland conditions as a female have had much to do with the decision to migrate, especially for single women. In the Basque diaspora, both women and men escaped political, economic, and social oppression in their search for a better life. Women also migrated to escape the various forms of oppression that are unique to their gender status. Many female interviewees stated that together with economic hardship in Euskal Herria, they had helped convince their husbands, brothers, and fathers to migrate. Furthermore, because many Basque women experienced economic and social status gain in their new host countries, they were not as motivated as their male counterparts to try to return to Euskal Herria. For economic as well as family reasons, then, two-thirds of the females responded that they now maintain their own lives in their host countries and plan to return to Euskal Herria only to visit. Thus for the typical female of the Basque diaspora, family obligation in the Basque Country has transformed into diaspora family obligation — the birth and raising of children and grandchildren — and further, she is now accustomed to the host country pace and lifestyle.

While some welcomed migration, a change in personal status might also be negative for a woman who was accustomed to the respect for motherhood and homemaking customary in the Basque Country, but with less status in the United States or Australia. They might also compare themselves less favorably to other immigrants in these host societies. Though much of the literature on the diaspora in South American communities emphasizes the importance of Basques in the elite social, economic and political structures, the views expressed in the aforementioned personal questionnaires paint a different picture. Barely one-fifth of the total respondents agreed that, "persons of Basque heritage have a higher socioeconomic status than other immigrants in (host country)." In Australia, where Basque ethnicity is unfamiliar and unknown, only 7% of the respondents agreed while the highest percentage in agreement with the statement (31%) came from the United States, where white European immigrants are generally granted higher status than people of Latino, Asian, or African origin. Basque women in all five countries do not perceive themselves as having a higher status than other immigrants.

Emigrant Basque women in all settings found themselves increasingly dependent on their children for communicating in a foreign language, dealing with school experiences and an outside culture that they were not as familiar with because they worked at home. This loss of self-esteem and self-assurance equated to a loss of identity for many women. Basque Centers often served as institutions where one could express oneself and understand the conversations and cultural con-

AMATXI, AMUMA, AMONA | 149

texts of activities. Latter-generation females, and especially
teenaged girls, reinforced this pattern through their lasting
friendships with other Basque girls. Teens who participated
in the dancing groups, choirs, and sporting sets, for example,
reaffirmed what their parents often hope for — they believe
their "Basque Center friends are friends for life." However,
with time and language skills improvement, women in all
age categories responded that they are comfortable with host
country friends, and only between 16% of the 18-30 years old
and 21% of the 76-90 years old women felt more comfortable
with their Basque friends.

Banal Nationalism and Daily Ethnic Socialization

The idea that home decoration and jewelry usage reinforce
ethnonationalist sentiment has been heretofore overlooked
as female triviality and therefore not worthy of academic research. However, I have found that both of these forms of expression recreate ethnic identity through the use of intimate
objects, thereby psychologically reinforcing ethnicity and
ethnic socialization for both the individual and her family. In
addition, they also demonstrate one's "Basqueness" to home
visitors and the public. The resurgence in the use of Basque
names for children is also prevalent and marks an obvious and
public ethnic boundary for those children for the rest of their
lives. It is another constant reminder, especially in English-
speaking societies, every time it is spelled, explained, and its
pronunciation corrected, that one is Basque.

House decoration tends to be the domain of the female
head of household, and in many of these cases non-Basque
women that married a Basque also tended to use ethnic symbolic objects in home decoration. A home provides the setting for modern intimacy and moral community. Values and
expectations are transmitted and intensified through which
specific types of objects are selected for display, and many

Basque women utilize their homes and home decoration to create and express their identity. Photographs of family and ancestors, family farmhouses and villages, punctuate the importance of descent and connection to the Basque Country. Mementos from tourist gift shops are, likewise, placed in areas of importance and displayed with care.

Carved wooden busts of *Amumas* (Grandmothers) and *Aitxitxes* (Grandfathers), Tree of Gernika artistic representations, coats of arms of the seven provinces of Euskal Herria, pictures of *txistulariak* (Basque flute players), and *ikurrinak* (Basque flags were, indeed, everywhere), greet visitors to thousands of Basque homes in the diaspora. This day-to-day reminding and remembering one's ancestors and ethnic identity creates an example of what social psychologist Michael Billig calls "banal nationalism." [89] The ordinary everyday habits, language, food, and displaying of cultural artifacts, to cite but a few examples, serve as a constant reminder to these families of their Basque heritage. Interviews in each of the five countries were conducted in Basque homes and the majority utilized ethnic cultural decoration. Though I was consciously looking for such material and noticed it quite easily, the Basques welcoming me into their homes specifically and affectionately pointed out their objects. They did this not to "prove" their Basqueness to me, but rather to emphasize the importance it represented to them.

Basque women utilize the *ikurrina's* red, green and white colors for a myriad of choices from linen to dress tables, to the painting of the house exteriors, and the colors of flowers to plant for the garden. Several women mentioned (without being prompted) that they will not plant red and yellow blooming flowers together because they are the colors of the Spanish flag. Whether in clothing, jewelry, or house decoration,

---

89   See Michael Billig, *Banal Nationalism* (London: Sage Publications, 1995).

because they do use quantities of green and red, many stated they seldom buy anything yellow just to ensure they never mistakenly put the two together. Everything from the choices of wedding and funeral flowers to furniture fabric and stoneware glaze seemed to be at least subconsciously affected by whether or not it might promote a Basque awareness. What remains conscious is the deliberate separation of red from yellow, the two colors that, combined, seem to trigger a negative response especially from emigrant and first generation, host country-born Basques.

Personal ornaments and jewelry have often been utilized as expressions of group identity with intense symbolic significance. In India, for example, there are rigid laws of caste that restrict the wearing of gold to people of certain groups only. [90] Within Basque communities, gold religious medals for baptisms or First Holy Communions are customary and although some of the younger interviewees stated they do not wear their medals regularly to host country social functions, they almost always wear them to similar Basque occasions. Men typically wear them inside their clothing, but women are more likely to display them outside of their apparel. *Lauburu* (a Basque symbol of a four-headed cross) emblem rings, earrings, and necklaces are also popular with males and females as are t-shirts, baseball caps, belt-buckles, and car bumper stickers with Basque themes. Several males in Australia and the United States even have permanently tattooed lauburus on their arms.

Besides public displays of Basqueness there are also those closer to the heart such as that of Juan Miguel Salaberry, an elderly gentleman from Rosario, Uruguay. For decades, Juan Miguel has worn his grandfather's *txapela* (beret) every day, and in his wallet has carried a small tattered paper *ikurrina*.

---

90 See Oppi Untracht, *Traditional Jewelry of India* (London: Thames and Hudson, 1997).

He says together they keep him safe. After migrating to Melbourne, Nekane Candino legally changed her given name from a Spanish "Rosarito" (Basque given names were not permitted in the four Spanish provinces during the Franco years) to the Basque "Nekane." This was self-actualizing for her because as she described herself, "Being Basque is primordial. There are thousands of years of Basqueness in me. I am not Nekane who also happens to be Basque. I am Basque and that shapes how I manifest myself as Nekane." These insignificant daily demonstrations of Basqueness may be "banal," "symbolic" or "leisure time ethnicity" to some academics, but for Juan Miguel and Nekane, as well as thousands more like them in the diaspora, maintaining Basque identity is not only a rational matter, but also one of great instinct, emotion, and spirit.

Ethnic identity is increasingly voluntary in the diaspora communities to which Basques have migrated. As Basques are not distinguishable by, for example, skin color, garments, or diet within these European settler countries, maintaining "Basqueness" becomes a choice. Basques are marking their own group identity boundaries rather than being marked by other outside groups, and the importance of naming provides a clear example of this phenomenon. Just as Nekane needed a Basque name to fulfill her identity, young parents of all generations are increasingly giving Basque first names to their children. There are numerous Mirens, Amaias, Nekanes, Idoias, and Maites, as well as Aitors, Kepas, Josus, Mikels, and Iñakis. In Australia and the United States special care must be given to how English-speaking people will pronounce (or mispronounce) a name, and the psychological impact that a unique name has on a child. As adults, interviewees stated that they were proud of their given and surnames, although as children a few hated them because of endless childhood teasing and the constant spelling and correction of pronunciation. In the Australian and United States societies, where it is customary for a woman to drop her surname and assume that of her husband,

Basque women in the last twenty years have increasingly refused to accept this practice and kept their maiden surnames
when marrying non-Basques. This serves as yet another constant demonstration and reminder of ethnic identity.

Conclusions

This mosaic of Basques in several diaspora communities demonstrates the slender differences between men and women
in their definitions of Basqueness, and the general similarities among women regardless of geography, age, and generation. That said, frequent exchange and recent migration
have meant that the Belgian community tends to be closer
to homeland ideas of what factors constitute being Basque,
whereas a certain distance, both temporal and spatial, marks
the cultural divide between United States Basques and these
same factors. As Euskal Herria has moved toward a more civic definition of including those people who live and work in
the Basque Country, and those who work for the culture and
indeed identify themselves as Basque, so the diaspora communities have tended to maintain a traditional conservative
approach to Basque ethnonationalist sentiment. The majority of these Basques are not interested in, and do not know
the details of, the political system of Spain's autonomous and
foral communities, for example, but are more interested in
preserving cultural aspects of their ethnicity, with the important exception of language (an ethnic marker that requires
perhaps a greater and more difficult degree of commitment
than other expressions of Basque ethnic identity).

Basque emigrant women have surmounted numerous life
altering experiences such as changing languages, cultures and
societies, and found strength in each other through Basque
Center activities. Ethnic identity is, therefore, not restricted

to those people who live inside a certain physical boundary and we can see, from thousands of Basques in the diaspora, that maintaining a connection to a specific ethnic identity is a personal choice. This is demonstrated from the wearing of *lauburu* earrings in Brussels to planting red-flowered gardens in Boise.

Euskadi — Venezuela: Natural Poetic Rapprochement

Matte Nuñez-Betelu

Recent developments in feminist thinking have encouraged new currents of thought in which not only the relationships between gender, race and sex are considered but also that of a new parameter, nature. This new branch, known as ecofeminism, seeks to study and establish links between the domination of women and that of nature. Different critics, such as Karen Warren, Val Plumwood, Maria Mies and Vandana Shiva, have underlined the parallel inferior role that both nature and women have been assigned and have played in relation to a superior role performed by the patriarchal model. Consequently, women have traditionally been related to nature just as men have been to reason and culture. Furthermore, within this sphere women and nature have been assigned a negative value whereas men and culture occupy the positive pole.

The above mentioned critics claim that the identification of woman and nature is a myth, an attempt to universalize a single concept of woman that fails to represent the complete picture of womanhood. Women and nature have been identified with one another due to a common bond of domination and exploitation. However, it should also be possible to look at the relationship of women and men to nature on their own terms. As Plumwood maintains:

> One essential feature of all ecological feminist positions is that they give positive value to a connection of women with nature which was previously, in the west, given a negative cultural value and which was the main ground of women's devaluation and oppression. Ecological feminists are involved in a great cultural revaluation of the status of women, the feminine and the natural, a revaluation which must recognize the way in which their historical connection in western culture has influenced the construction of the feminine identity. [91]

Accordingly, the purpose of this article is to explore the role that nature, and particularly landscape, plays in several selected poems by a Basque woman and poet, Balendiñe Albizu. From an ecofeminist perspective, I intend to analyze the way in which Albizu challenges a traditional male concept of the world: first, by adopting the task of political instigator which traditionally does not become a woman; and second, by allying herself with nature in an attempt to break the barriers imposed by men and re-map the world according to her ethnic and cultural restlessness rather than to geographically constructed determination. Albizu creates a poetic rapprochement between Euskadi and Venezuela using the natural elements in landscape as a political tool.

Albizu's work carries a strong and radical political message. In fact, many of her poems explicitly demand independence for the Basque Country as the only way to achieve her ultimate goal: the revival and survival of the Basque language and culture. In *Green Voices* (1995) Terry Gifford emphasizes the importance of using natural imagery by claiming that "there can be no 'innocent' reference to nature in a poem. Any reference will implicitly or explicitly express a notion of

---

91 Val Plumwood, *Feminism and the Mastery of Nature* (New York: Routledge, 1993), p. 8.

nature that relates to culturally developed assumptions about metaphysics, aesthetics, politics and status, that is in many cases, ideologies." [92] As Albizu's poems demonstrate, her use of landscape ultimately serves a politically inspired plan.

In order to reinforce her ideas every element of the poetry becomes a political tool. Nature is no exception since, as Plumwood reminds us, "the treatment of nature can be thought of in political terms as well as ethical terms," concluding that, "human relationships to nature are not only ethical, but also political." [93] Therefore while Albizu recognizes ethical questions surrounding the treatment of nature, she principally employs natural imagery as a mechanism to achieve the political agenda her poetry seeks to spread. Consequently, Albizu shapes nature in a politically motivated way since, in her poetry, all elements are political.

I will examine a series of poems which follow this trajectory. These poems begin with Civil War battles in the mountains of Euskadi. Later she locates her poetic voice in Venezuela, from where she keeps looking back to the natural space she left behind. Although she is not in Euskadi anymore, she still remembers her familiar natural surroundings: the mountains, the sea, and the flora. However, she slowly begins to feel the presence of the Venezuelan landscape, gradually integrating her old environment into the new one surrounding her. As such, she ultimately recognizes elements of what she left behind in Euskadi in what she has now in Venezuela. Actual independence is not achieved by the mere use of her poems but she succeeds in creating, through nature, a real geographical and cultural space from which to keep Basque culture alive. This space is created through establishing a natural poetic rapprochement between Venezuela and Euskadi.

92   Terry Gifford, *Green Voices: Understanding Contemporary Nature Poetry* (Manchester: Manchester University Press, 1995), p. 16.

93   Plumwood, *Feminism and the Mastery of Nature*, pp. 2, 13.

Landscape is pivotal in Albizu's work. The critic Chris Fitter explains that "in order to reconstruct as fully as possible the landscape-consciousness of an earlier poet, we must outstep the limits of the text and endeavor to reconstruct its enabling cognitive world." [94] Personal experience, both of political events as well as of moments in nature, clearly acquire great importance in the poems of Albizu. Thus, in order to understand her poetic evolution it is necessary, as Fitter implies, to explore first the recent historical events that Spain and the Basque Country experienced and the way Albizu lived these initial moments of political involvement in a male dominated world.

The Spanish Civil War (1936-1939) erupted out of a general political turmoil that engulfed Spain during the 1930s. The bitter and destructive nature of the war forced many sympathizers of the losing side, including many Basques, into exile. Balendiñe Albizu (Zumaia, 1914) was one of those Basques who, after fighting against Franco's Nationalist forces, left the country for Venezuela where she remained until 1995. However, her struggle did not end on the new continent. In renewing the cause, however, she chose a different weapon: poetry. On arriving in Venezuela, Albizu poured the ideals she had fought for back home into her poems, using them as another way of challenging the Franco regime from her exile.

The political situation in Spain precluded many of her poems from being published in the Basque Country. In fact, most of them were not directed to an Old World audience but to the Basque diaspora. Her poems, therefore, quickly inspired and instructed a new generation of Venezuelan-born new Basques, who found in her poetry a link with the land of their ancestors. Albizu not only created this link but she also

---

94   Chris Fitter, *Poetry, Space and Landscape* (Cambridge: Cambridge University Press, 1995), p. 2.

actively sought out her reader's identification with the homeland. Venezuela's first role in this task is that of a safe haven.
At the same time, Albizu's task is to create a bridge between
both harbors through her poetry.

When the war broke out in 1936, the confrontation divided Spain in two. Almost immediately, two groups were
formed: the Republicans and the Nationalists. The Republicans defended the constitutional regime of the Second Republic. Led by Franco, the Nationalists considered their military
uprising as a crusade to save Spain from her enemies, namely
the left and minorities such as Basques and Catalans. The
Basque Country was no exception to the struggle although
there it took a slightly different twist: the Nation that was to
be saved was not Spain but the Basque Country. During the
course of the Second Republic the Basque Provinces seemed
to be on their way to gaining some form, however limited,
of autonomy. Yet the outbreak of the war obviously endangered this situation and many Basques thought this to be the
appropriate moment to seek an independence that would put
an end to the insecurity provided by a dubious form of autonomy.[95]

Most of the information about Albizu's involvement in
the war comes from the introduction to each of her three collections of poetry compiled in *Olerkiak* (Poems) (1984), and
from Elixabete Garmendia's book, *Balendiñe Albizu* (1998). In
the introduction to *Olerkiak,* the compiler, Father Onaindia,
gives a brief biographical account from which one can infer a
very active role in the conflict. Born into a Basque Nationalist
family, when Franco's Nationalist troops were about to take
her hometown of Zumaia in September 1936, Albizu and her
brothers fled on a ship where she was the only woman. After
losing contact with her brothers, she arrived in Bilbao where

---

95   Martín de Ugalde, *Síntesis de la historia del País Vasco* (Barcelona:
Ediciones Vascas, 1977), p. 207.

she joined the forces of the Basque resistance government. According to Garmendia, Albizu's job at that time consisted of feeding, cleaning and nurturing the soldiers from the Amaiur Batallion. [96] As Franco's forces advanced, Albizu fled from one city to another. With the fall of Bilbao in June 1937, she abandoned the Basque Country for neighboring Santander, but when this, too, was on the point of capitulation, she fled to France where the Basque government had set up its exiled headquarters. Finally, in 1940, when all hope of returning to the Basque Country had diminished, she took a ship to Venezuela along with her husband and her baby.

Basque exiles in Caracas formed a rather numerous and active community. There, Albizu frequented the Eusko Etxea or Basque Club in the Venezuelan capital. This served not only as a meeting place for Basques in exile, but also sponsored and promoted different cultural activities. Many of these were directed towards the preservation of the Basque language in their Spanish-speaking surroundings. As part of these activities, for example, the club launched several magazines such as *Euskadi, Euzko Gaztedi, Sabindarra* and *Irrintzi* [97] and within those pages Albizu pursued her political cause in favor of Basque nationalism. In the articles and poems for these magazines Albizu vividly described the lives of Basque refugees and, even more importantly for this community, transmitted a feeling that the Basque cause was not entirely lost. Many Basques had died fighting for freedom but their country was now subdued by the Franco dictatorship. So that the blood of those who died should not have been shed in vain, argued Albizu, the struggle must continue until Basques achieved their ultimate goal of independence. This is a message that her poems repeat time and time again, as in "Euskaldunak" (Basques) (1975): *"Geure-geuria dan Euskalerria /*

96   Elixabete Garmendia, *Balendiñe Albizu* (Vitoria-Gasteiz: Eusko Jaurlaritzaren Argitalpen Zerbitzu Nagusia, 1998), p. 7.

97   Ibid., p. 13.

bakar-bakarrik nai degu / izan dedilla geure-geurea" (The only thing we want / is that our Euskalerria / be really ours). [98] Similarly, in the 1971 poem "Eusko gazteak" (Basque Youth), the struggle for freedom provides the dominant message:

> Askatasuna da guk nai deguna,
> askatasuna nai degu azi,
> askatasunaz erriak bizi,
> eskuak lotuta, lo-lo, ezin bizi
>
> (We want freedom,
> we want to grow up free,
> we want people to live free,
> we cannot live handcuffed, asleep) [99]

More than 30 years after Albizu first began writing for the magazines published by the Eusko Etxea of Caracas, some of these early poems, as well as other unpublished material, appeared in a single collection. This was published in the Basque Country in 1972 under the tide, *Nere olerki txorta* (My Poetry Collection). Two years later, a second work, *Nere bideetan* (On My Travels) was compiled in Caracas but ultimately never published. Finally, in 1984 the previously mentioned *Olerkiak* appeared. This book included the two previous collections as well as a third, entitled *Nere biotz-dardarak* (My Heartbeats), and coupled poems previously published in the magazines of the Eusko Etxea with new and original work.

All three books share a profound love for the Basque Country as well as a sense of responsibility towards the Basque cause. However, the general tone of the poetry changes from one work to another, and this is especially evident between the first two and the third books. Only a few of the poems in *Nere Olerki txorta* are dated and the only date offered is 1944-45. In *Nere bideetan,* although two of the poems are dated 1936 and

---

98   Balendiñe Albizu, *Olerkiak* (Bilbao: Igarri, 1984), p. 223.

99   Ibid., p. 218.

1953 respectively, the rest are from 1971 to 1974. *Nere biotz-dardarak,* however, spans a longer period from 1936 to 1982. As both the dates and topics of the poems overlap in the three different collections — they were written at the same time although published at different periods — I will consider them all as a single collection, that is, as the final book *Olerkiak.* In order to show the poetical rapprochement her poems achieve, instead of following the order they appear in the book, I will follow the date (when given) or the particular message that they convey.[100]

The first dated poems are included in a section called "Guda aldiko kezkak" (Wartime Concerns) where Albizu explores the personal meaning and consequences of war. This section has a clearly political and propagandistic tone,[101] and includes the largest body of poems about the Civil War itself. Indeed several were written while the conflict still raged on, between 1936 and 1937.

In some cases, Albizu presents the same moment from a different perspective every time. In "Gudaren asiera" (The Beginning of the War, 1936), for example, she denounces divisions among Basques as a result of the conflict and calls for unity, a call she will repeat in many other poems. As a result, this piece transmits a sense of fear and insecurity. In "Euzkadin, gudaren asieran" (In the Basque Country, at the Beginning of the War, 1936) she again describes the outbreak of hostilities but this time, instead of centering on fear or uncertainty, she celebrates the courage of Basque soldiers who

---

100 Not all of Albizu's poems have been taken into account, but rather those that reflect her poetic rapprochement. *Olerkiak* includes many religious poems, as well as several dedicated to her children and grandchildren. For the sake of consistency with my thesis of poetic rapprochement, they have not been considered here.

101 Although written after 1936, most of these poems were not published in Spain until 1982, well after Franco's death. Before that date (Spanish government censorship continued even after the death of Franco in 1975), such a propagandists: tone would have been unthinkable.

bravely go to fight singing war songs. Nevertheless, the optimism of the first lines soon disappears and the poem ends with a note of rancor, "Ainbeste kalte, ai euskaldunak! / nola aztu ta barkatu.. .!"(So much damage, oh Basques! / how can we forget and forgive).[102]

With the passage of time Albizu begins to reflect on the consequences of the conflict, in particular condemning the misery that war had brought. In "Guda maltzurra" (Pernicious War) human suffering is reflected in nature when she states:

Sutan gure mendi,
baso, uri ta erri,
su-garraren artean
millaka gudari

(Burning mountains,
forests, cities and towns,
thousands of warriors
among the flames)[103]

By locating warriors and nature on the same stage, Albizu establishes a common struggle for the two of them. At the same time, they are both being attacked and she does not hesitate to find a culprit: "Españak beti guri / kalte digu ekarri" (Spain has always / brought us damage).[104] This is but one example of the animosity Albizu feels for the country, since it was Spain that had brought misery to both the people and land.

However, war is not always treated with that rancorous tone that these early poems displayed. This is more than evident when Albizu chooses to praise valor. Indeed, "Nere anai txikien Josu" (My Youngest Brother Josu) praises the individ-

---

102   Albizu, *Olerkiak,* p. 206.

103   Ibid., p. 207.

104   Ibid., p. 207.

ual courage of warriors like her seventeen-year-old brother who died in the war. The poem, far from showing pain or hate against the killers, conveys a sense of pride towards the teenager's actions. At the same time, she again uses nature as a backdrop:

> Urkiola mendian
> burruka gogorrean
> gudariekin batean
> bizia eman zenduan
>
> (On the mountain of Urkiola
> in a fierce fight
> you gave your life
> like one of the warriors) [105]

In this case she does not reflect on the suffering of nature but at the same time, her brother does not seem to suffer either. Ultimately the poem expresses a moment of heroism in which there is no room for suffering. Collective bravery is shown in poems like "Guda Eresia" (War Elegy). Once again, the warrior is located within a natural framework:

> Euskaldun gazte auek
> mendi gaillurretan
> ziñ egin zuten denak,
> gudako egunetan,
> ez da etsaia sartuko
> ez, gure errietan...
>
> (These young Basques
> atop the mountains
> they all swore
> during the days of war
> that the enemy will not enter
> our towns) [106]

---

105   Ibid., p. 208.

106   Ibid., p. 209.

The mountains that witness their oath are the same ones that take them in since "Antxe gelditu ziñaten / gure lur maite ortan / betiko geienak" (There remained / most of you forever / in our beloved land). [107] Once more, the identification of warrior with land is evident. Thus nature is conceived in different ways depending on Albizu's intentions. If she wants to underline human suffering, nature suffers too, but when people's bravery is exalted, natural elements appear in all their magnificence. Diego Marín, author of *Poesía Paisajística Española: 1940 – 1970* (1976) studies a group of poems written in the same period as Albizu's and, on contemplating the theme of nature, concludes that "el paisaje está visto en función del estado anímico." [108] This seems to be true of Albizu, too, as she clearly adopts a standard Romantic posture towards nature.

In most of her war poems, Albizu repeats and denounces constantly the injustice of the situation in an attempt to make the world see things as she does. Consequently, her later poems show that, although the war has been over for a long time, the fight, for Albizu, is not over. She repeats in her poetry those glorious moments in which the Basque people resisted Franco's forces. However, with the passage of time, she targets a different audience. Her poems begin to reflect the reality of the moment and the place in which she is living, and she finds a new readership in the Basque youth of Venezuela.

One might argue that the poems mentioned thus far did not have a specific audience but rather a goal, the propagation of the Basque Nationalist fight. However, with time we increasingly find a series of poems directly devoted to the Basque youth of Venezuela. For example, the previously mentioned "Eusko gazteak" (Basque Youth) lauds young, Caracas-

---

107   Ibid.

108   Diego Marín, *Poesía paisajística española: 1940—1970. Estudio y antología* (London: Tamesis Books Ltd, 1979), p. 29.

born Basques, and calls these young people to join forces and free the Basque Country. Specifically she implores: "elkartu gaitezen gazte guztiok / guazen Euzkadi askatzera" (Let's all get together / let's set Euzkadi free). [109] In "'Eusko [110] Etxeko' euzko gaztedia" (Basque Youth of the Basque Club) and "'Euzko-gaztedia'-n ezi ta oretutako eusko gaztea gaur, eredu da" (Basque Youth Raised in the Basque Club Today, an Example), she once again praises the young in Caracas and their efforts to keep the language and culture alive. Albizu fears that the Basque Country will lose its essence as it is in danger of being absorbed by Spanish culture. Therefore her plan, it seems, is to keep Basque culture alive in Venezuela and, somehow, transfer it back to the Basque Country at an appropriate moment.

All these poems underline the importance Albizu gives to her homeland in terms of the political fight she defends. However, a different kind of poem shows her appreciation of the Basque Country in a less political way. [111] Some of the poems, then, in the two other collections *(Nere olerki txorta* and *Nere bideetan)* recall the past as an idealized, better time. In "San Telmo Kalea" (San Telmo Street), Albizu relates happiness to places where she lived, familiar landmarks, or special moments: "San Telmo eguna / nere kaleko pestak / neretzat egunik pozgarrienak" (The day of San Telmo / festivities in my street / the happiest day for me). [112] Amid these past memories, natural elements are not only part of the preparations for the festivities — "Gure kalea apaintzen gendun / paper, belar, iri ta lore" (We used to decorate our street / paper, grass and flowers) — but they are also part of her everyday life:

109   Albizu, *Olerkiak*, p. 218.

110   Albizu constantly switches from "s" to "z" in words like *euzko / eusko* and *Euzkadi / Euskadi*. I have kept her original spelling.

111   I am referring here to the absence of an explicit political *message* in these poems. There remains the political *use* of nature, which will serve to create the poetic rapprochement I am highlighting in the argument.

112   Albizu, *Olerkiak*, p. 26.

gau ixillean,
itxaspeko olatuaren
zurru-murrua entzuten nuen
nere gelatik oeratzean.
Nere irudiz seaska abestia
olatuaren jun da etorria

(in the quiet night
I used to hear the murmur
of the waves in the sea.
The waves coming and going
were for me as a lullaby) [113]

Nature, therefore, seems to have been an integral part of her life when she lived in the Basque Country, but what about Venezuela?

Another section in the book, entitled "Ipar eta Egoaldetik" (From the North and the South), reveals the increasing importance Albizu gives to her new land. Although most of the poems considered so far were written in Caracas, Albizu ignored Venezuela and looked almost exclusively to the Basque Country. Even those dedicated to young Venezuelans were devoted to making them value the Basque Country instead of Venezuela. Nevertheless, within this new group of poems, we see a change. While still consumed by the Basque Country, Albizu increasingly invokes Venezuela in order to create a bridge between both countries. Not surprisingly, this link is provided by nature.

In several instances, Albizu uses an ocean metaphor to bring her homeland near, equating the Venezuelan Caribbean to the Basque Cantabrian Sea. In "Itxasoaren gora-beherak. Kantauri ta Karibe" (The Ebb and Flow of the Sea. Cantabrian and Caribbean) she finds an affinity among those who have been born by the ocean:

---

113   Ibid., p. 27.

Itxas ertzean jaio geranak [sic]
benetan degu maitatzen,
bere aunditasunak,
zoratzen gaitu,
ta, ezin bizi bera gabe

(Those of us who have been born
by the sea we truly love it,
its magnitude
enthralls us,
and, we cannot live without it) [114]

Albizu thus breaks down the frontiers between countries, creating a fraternal sense among all those united by the sea. Similarly, in "Orinoko ibaia" (The Orinoco River) she also demonstrates admiration and respect for the beautiful river that flows into the Atlantic Ocean, the same one that eventually will reach the Basque Country.

The sea provides the connection between both continents. Still, Albizu's object of desire was at the far end of the bridge. Little by little, her poems will start to reveal not only what lies within her memory but also what she sees before her own eyes. Just as she used landscape to relate to happy moments in her past, so she gradually incorporated similar imagery to describe her present. In "Ikuspenak" (Visibility) she records what she sees every day from the window of her house in Venezuela, namely, birds flying over nearby Mount Avila, transmitting a feeling of happiness and peace.

The same mountain will inspire another of her poems, "Avila mendiko gurutzeari" (To the Cross of Mount Avila). This time, however, the poem becomes a prayer as she asks the cross on the mountain to bring peace to humanity. If we agree with Marin that, "al paisaje físico se superpone por aso-

---

114   Ibid., p. 38.

ciación afectiva el evocado" [115] then we might conclude that the cross on this mountain is symbolic of another famous one in the Basque Country, the Cross of Mount Gorbea, which has inspired many popular songs. However, the fact that crosses crown many mountains in Euskadi, and that no specific reference to another mountain is made in the poem, ultimately means that Albizu is validating the Venezuelan landmark.

Landscape, then, together with the connection between people and nature, provides a first link in Albizu's poetic rapprochement. As we have seen, some of her poems dedicated to the Basque youth of Venezuela considered them solely as potential liberators of Euskadi. As such, Venezuela was but a greenhouse that permitted the unchallenged growth of Basque seeds. Gradually, however, Albizu begins to see them as Venezuelan-born Basques, that is, as Basques of the diaspora. She thus redirects her original goal. Since she cannot be in the Basque Country working for the development of Basque culture there, she will engage in the same activity in Venezuela.

"Caracasko ikastolako umeak" (The Children of the Caracas Ikastola) praises children who, despite living in a different culture, still make an effort to retain their ancestral heritage. Along the same lines, "Lintxu" talks about a young Venezuelan woman who was so impressed by Basque culture that she learned Euskera and eventually moved to the Basque Country, where she lived until her death. However, Albizu muses that she will always be alive in their hearts. She also dedicates a poem to William Douglass, an American anthropologist from the University of Nevada, for his important work in spreading the learning of the language and culture. All these poems seem to express the author's idea that while the language is being persecuted in the Basque Country under Franco's dictatorship (1939 − 1975), the rest of the world

115   Marín, *Poesía paisajística española*, p. 29.

should serve as the cradle from which to nurture it. At the same time, this implies a conception of a world without frontiers, where everybody can feel at home anywhere.

This leads to the question of how she identifies Venezuela and Euskadi. The identification is achieved in two progressive steps, each one determined to end the circular trajectory of her poetry. Firstly, Albizu began her poetic activity by addressing the theme of war. Several years later, she begins to identify the war that she suffered in Euskadi in 1936 with the Venezuelan wars against Spain that ultimately led to independence in 1829. Although the South American wars took place more than a century before the Spanish civil war,

Albizu sees many parallels between the two struggles, especially that of having a common enemy: Spain. As a result, several poems praise the battle of Carabobo, a decisive battle in the Venezuelan struggle for independence from the Spanish. One such poem compares it to the battle of Artxanda, an important Basque rearguard action during the Spanish Civil War. In both cases, the battle took place in the mountains, and the mountains remain a symbol of the warriors' bravery. As the central theme of Albizu's poetry is direct confrontation (be this political or cultural), she is now conscious of similar historical struggles in her new environment.

Secondly, she will bring the Basque Country to Venezuela. For example, in her poem, "Euzkadiren zortzigarren erria" (The Eighth Province of Euskadi) she declares Venezuela as part of the Basque Country by stating:

> Ez dakit zeñek esana da au...
> — Zortzi-erri ditula Euskadik;
> Aberri barruan dim zazpi,
> ta, ludian zear bat, ara zortzi —

(I don't know who said this:
Euskadi has eight provinces;
seven are in the homeland
and, across the world,
there's number eight) [116]

Venezuela thus becomes part of that province scattered around the globe. In fact, Albizu poetically remaps the world to frame one united diasporic entity. In effect, all those Basque communities outside the geographical frontiers of Euskadi form the eighth province. Belonging to the eighth province is determined by cultural and ethnic affirmation rather than by politically established geographical location.

Albizu's most repeated message is that of independence for the Basque Country. In this sense, politically speaking, she fails to see her dream come true. Linguistically, however, she is successful by creating a space in her poems in which one can freely exercise his/ her right to live as a Basque. Her poems become more than merely political propaganda on account of the use she makes of nature. Nature helps her to create a new space that she then fills with words. As opposed to man, nature defies the rules of politics and civilization. As opposed to the state, Albizu defies the same rules. Nature recognizes no frontiers since it encompasses the world. As such, Albizu cannot understand the partition that the Spanish and French states impose on her land.

By looking at nature, she realizes she can see the same things — the sea, the mountains, or the rivers — from any point of the globe. And the global truth is that one mountain leads to another, and another, and another until reaching the one she originally had in mind. Nature thus provides a continuum that war and men have broken. However, Albizu restores that continuum by boldly affirming: "Emendik ikusiko

---

116   Albizu, *Olerkiak*, p. 128.

ditut gaur / nere erriko maiteko pestak / ikusi bai, begiak itxita (From here today onwards I will see / the festivities of my beloved country / yes, I'll see them, just by closing my eyes). [117] "Emendik" (From here) refers to Venezuela while "nere erriko maiteko pestak" (the festivities of my beloved country) are obviously those of the Basque Country. The distance between both is non-existent. This is the power that nature brings to Albizu's work, the power to exercise an actual poetic rapprochement.

---

117   Ibid., p. 27.

The Tragedy of Yoyes

Cameron J. Watson

I don't want to become a woman that, just because men consider me in some way tough, is accepted. How can I make my presence help other women to feel like this? How can I make my presence call out to other women and not make others think of me, in some way, as a rare species? How can I make these men understand that women's liberation is a revolutionary goal so that they fully understand?. . . How can I blend the revolution with women's liberation?[118]

Introduction

Women remain absent from most studies of Basque political violence. This, I suspect, has something to do with the tabooed nature of the topic itself,[119] so that women's involvement in the "dangerous" world of terrorism is typically reduced to broad stereotypical (and often sexual) images.[120] Within the history of Basque political violence one woman cannot be ignored from serious scholarship: Maria Dolores González Katarain, or "Yoyes" as she was more commonly known. A

118   María Dolores González Katarain [Yoyes, pseud.] (February 1978), quoted in Elixabete Garmendia Lasa *et al, Yoyes. Desde su ventana* (Iruñea: Garrasi, 1987), p. 57, cited in Miren Alcedo, "Mujeres de ETA: La cuestión del genero en la clandestinidad," *La Factoía,* no. 4 (October 1997). At http://www.aquibaix.com/factoria/articulos/ miren4.htm

119   Cf. Joseba Zulaika and William A. Douglass, *Terror and Taboo: The Follies, Fables, and Faces of Terrorism* (New York and London: Routledge, 1996), pp. 152-54.

120   Cf. Cameron Watson, "Imagining ETA," in *Basque Politics and Nationalism,* ed. William A. Douglass, Carmelo Urza, Linda White, and Joseba Zulaika. (Reno: Basque Studies Program, 1999), pp. 94-114.

leader of ETA *{Euskadi ta Askatasuna* — Basque Country and Freedom) in the 1970s, Yoyes subsequently relinquished her position in the organization to go into a self-imposed exile at the end of the decade. Returning to the Basque Country in the mid 1980s under a Spanish government amnesty, she was shot dead by the very organization she had led just a few years before.

The present article has a threefold argument. Firstly, I contend that the historiography of Basque nationalism in general, and more specifically that of ETA, has undervalued the role that Yoyes played in leading the organization during the mid and late 1970s. Secondly, I believe that the figure of Yoyes has been historically appropriated to *represent* different political ideologies, at the expense of forgetting the afore-mentioned role. Finally, I would contend that the story of Yoyes reveals the tragic nature of the Basque political experience during recent historical memory.

Youth 1954–1971

María Dolores González Katarain was born on May 14, 1954 in Ordizia (Gipuzkoa), the central market town of the *Goier-rior.* Basque highlands, perhaps *the* repository of *euskara* (the Basque language) and traditional culture within the social, economic and political upheavals affecting Basque society during the Spanish dictatorship of General Franco (1939-75).

> These natural borders . . . for hundreds of years separated this region of the Basque country from its neighbors, and sheltered its language and culture from the influence of immigrants, few of whom ever settled there . . . [however] since the industrial boom in the area in the 1950s, the population [grew] at the rate of about 3 percent annually, doubling about once every generation. The results of this demo-

> graphic explosion [were] disastrous for the quality
> of life of the region . . . [Yet] Euskera [was] still the
> dominant language . . . The confluence of all these
> forces . . . produced an unusual blend of traditional
> and modern in the lives of its residents. [121]

The second of eight children, Yoyes grew up amid this tremendous social transformation. Her mother, Angelita Katarain, had married Luis González who, although also from
Ordizia, was of Spanish descent. The couple owned a general
store in Ordizia and Yoyes later recalled with some sense of
irony that her father had always been an *españolista*, [122] or in
favor of the regime that had offered him some degree of economic opportunity outside his native province. With a large
family to support on the modest income of a small shop, Yoyes grew up among humble economic surroundings.

Together with modest economic beginnings the González
Katarain children (and others) also experienced a degree
of social marginality through their primary ethnic identity. [123]6 In a family of mixed parents, Basque and non-Basque,
there were, from the outset, two identities that Yoyes had to
contend with. Although she viewed her dual cultural heritage
as an enriching, rather than constricting, personal legacy, [124]
she had no doubts as to her "national" allegiance. She took her
primary Basque identity from her (Basque-speaking) mother,
as well as from her *cuadrilla*.

---

121   Robert P. Clark, *The Basque Insurgents: ETA, 1952-1980* (Madison:
The University of Wisconsin Press, 1984), pp. 198-202.

122   Anne Echeverry, "Mon amie Yoyes," in Various Authors, *Yoyes
1986-1996* (n.p.: Yoyesen Lagunak, 1996), p. 25.

123   Cf. the argument of Alfonso Pérez-Agote that, effectively, to be
Basque in Franco's Spain was to be roundly stigmatized. See *La repro-
ducción del nacionalismo. El caso vasco* (Madrid: Centro de Investigaciones
Sociológicas/Siglo XXI, 1984).

124   Echeverry, "Mon amie Yoyes," p. 25.

The *cuadrilla* is a group of friends in Basque society, the members of which, typically, form while they are still young children, share a common social and economic background and political outlook, and organize communal activities. *Cuadrillas* are sustained by a kind of balanced reciprocity, so while there is often a commonly acknowledged central figure, great care is taken not to over-emphasize that person's role, for in theory the group is based on communal equality. *Cuadrillas* thus tend to be closed and exclusive while at the same time communally supportive and, when occasion calls, easily mobilized.[125]

According to "Loli," a friend and member of Yoyes' *cuadrilla* (and also a member of ETA during the 1970s), "we were the children of those who had lost the Civil War. And that was something that dominated our lives . . . for us there was total repression." Similarly, another *cuadrilla* friend and future activist of ETA, "Koldo" recalled that he

> joined ETA because I became politically aware from the age of sixteen. I realized just how much my people were suffering from the suppression of our culture and language, especially our language. I felt this in my bones. I was not prepared for there to be a genocide of my culture. I was very much aware of this and I entered ETA to give it everything I had.[126]

Koldo, together with the quietest and most enigmatic member of the group, "Pakito" (Francisco Mujika Garmendia), would later form the link between Yoyes' *cuadrilla* and ETA.

---

125   Ander Gurruchaga, *El código nacionalista vasco durante el franquismo* (Barcelona: Anthropos, 1985), p. 364; Marianne Heiberg, *The Making of the Basque Nation* (Cambridge: Cambridge University Press, 1989), pp. 154-59.

126   Both appear in the BBC Television documentary "States of Terror: The Organisation," originally broadcast in 1993.

Yet just as Yoyes was in many ways a typical adolescent girl growing up in rural Gipuzkoa in the 1960s, something also set her apart. For example, she developed an appetite for feminist literature and more universal social questions beyond the political situation of Euskal Herria (the Basque Country). "I read [Simone de Beauvoir's] *The Second Sex*" she later recalled,

> at about age sixteen or seventeen. What a thrill! I could not believe that anyone could teach me so much, convince me with so many arguments and such clarity of so many self intuitions that I did not even dare contemplate for fear of seeming excessively strange in the environment in which I lived. I was right! I discovered even more! Later I sought out and always devoured all of her things fearful of finishing. [127]

The influence of de Beauvoir is important for two reasons. Firstly, it reveals the continuing importance of post-World War Two existentialism in defining radical Basque nationalism. I have argued elsewhere that existentialism played an extremely important, if subsequently undervalued, role in the intellectual formation of ETA in the 1950s. [128] ETA was formed in 1959 on the existentialist assumption that the Basque "essence" was not given, but rather that it had to be created through specific deeds rather than mere words. As de Beauvoir's lover, Jean-Paul Sartre, once observed, "existentialism defines man [and woman] by action." [129] It is interest-

---

127   María Dolores González Katarain [Yoyes, pseud.], diary entry, April 15, 1986, "Fragmentos de su diario" in Various Authors, *Yoyes 1986-1996*, p. 60.

128   See Cameron J. Watson, "Sacred Earth, Symbolic Blood: A Cultural History of Basque Political Violence From Arana to ETA," Ph.D. Diss, University of Nevada, Reno, 1996.

129   Jean-Paul Sartre, "A More Precise Characterization of Existentialism," *in Action* (December 1944), cited in *The Writings of Jean-Paul Sartre*, vol. 2, *Selected Prose*, ed. Michel Contat and Michel Rybalka, trans. Rich-

ing to note that Yoyes, a leader of ETA in the mid 1970s and from a significantly different socio-economic and educational background than the original founders of ETA, was also inspired by existentialist literature. Indeed, we might contend that, at least to some extent, the differences between successive generations of ETA leaders might not be so decisive as previously thought.

Secondly, Yoyes was clearly inspired by de Beauvoir in a consciously political way. If we understand, then, her role within ETA as significant to the direction of the organization, it is tempting to speculate about the contribution of feminist thought to radical Basque nationalism. "To pose women," argued de Beauvoir in *The Second Sex,* "is to pose the absolute Other, without reciprocity, denying against all experience that she is a subject, a fellow human being."[130] We might reasonably conclude that existential feminism bequeathed to Yoyes an especially acute awareness of the force of social stigma-tization. For her own dual identity, as both a Basque and a woman, must have made her doubly aware of the social status of *otherness* in Francoist Spain.

On the one hand, as Pérez-Agote argues (see note 6), during the Franco regime (1939-75) all expressions of Basque identity were roundly stigmatized. At the same time, then, just as the regime sought to eliminate — politically and culturally — Basque identity, so it also promoted a conservative and regressive patriarchal social project that projected womanhood as passive, pious and pure. Indeed if, as Helen Graham contends, "the Franco regime's object, similar to that of Italian and German fascism, was to obliterate women as independent

ard McCleary (Evanston: Northwestern University Press, 1974), p. 157.

130 Simone de Beauvoir, *The Second Sex,* trans. and ed. H.M. Parshley (New York: Alfred A. Knopf, 1964), p. 253.

social beings," [131] then we might trace a similarity with the kind of ideology behind the politico-cultural policies of the dictatorship towards Basques in general. As a consequence, radical Spanish nationalism, as expressed through the Franco regime, forcibly attempted to create a mono-cultural and ultra-conservative socially Catholic state. As such, for many Basque women, we might conclude that a rebellion against the condition of passive womanhood was, in fact, a rebellion against the condition of being Spanish itself.

In an important study on the nature of radical Basque nationalist militancy, Miren Alcedo Moneo seems to support this idea by suggesting that Yoyes may have sought a primary identity through her membership in the ETA. In a diary entry from 1984, for example, she recalled that she "did not know that once one gets seriously 'lost', the risk of never 'finding' oneself is truly great." [132] Yoyes' own militancy in ETA, therefore, potentially reveals an existential quest for self, for a personal identity refracted through both nationality and gender and ritually expressed in the membership of an organization dedicated to direct action.

Militancy 1971–1979

In 1971 Yoyes enrolled in the Escuela de Magisterio (Teacher Training College) in the capital of her native province, Donostia (San Sebastián). During that first year she joined a *talde* or clandestine pro-ETA group led by an active militant, whose members, although sympathetic to the cause, were not

---

131   Helen Graham, "Gender and the State: Women in the 1940s," in Helen Graham and Jo Labanyi, eds. *Spanish Cultural Studies: An Introduction: The Struggle for Modernity* (Oxford: Oxford University Press, 1995), p. 184.

132   Yoyes, quoted in Garmendia Lasa *et al, Desde su ventana*, p. 164, cited in Miren Alcedo Moneo, *Militar en ETA. Historias de vida y muerte* (Donostia-San Sebastián: Haranburu, 1996), p. 260.

expected to take any active part in ETA actions. Rather, these groups served as a form of introduction to the aims and ideals of ETA. "The members of [Yoyes'] *talde*" remembered Koldo, "were all girls. It was the first all-girl *talde* in the area, something rare at that time."[133] Soon after, Koldo and Pakito secretly met with ETA representatives in Donostia to discuss their wish to join the group. After the meeting it was decided that for the various members of their *cuadrilla* who wished to formally join ETA, some practical guidance was necessary. This would be provided by Juan Miguel Goiburu Mendizabal ("Goiherri"), an ETA member also from Ordizia, although a few years older than Yoyes and her friends. "I was from a previous generation," recalled Goiherri,

> and from an earlier stage of ETA. After the police actions against ETA in the early seventies there were very few of us left. We came across each other because we were from the same village and these people wanted political and cultural guidance to be politically active. Since I was already in the organization we were able to be very useful to one another.[134]

Loli later observed that,

> Juan Miguel had always known all of us in the *cuadrilla*. When we were young several of his *cuadrilla* used to take us up to the mountains and we saw a lot of him around the village. Later on, when he'd become involved in ETA, he'd actually carried out a recruitment drive and our *cuadrilla* was good recruiting ground.[135]

---

133   Koldo, cited in Garmendia Lasa *et al, Desde su ventana,* p. 32.

134   "States of Terror" (BBC Television).

135   Ibid.

During this time, then, ETA was quite clearly woven into the social fabric of Basque culture. It both fed and was sustained by the society from which it emerged.

After the initial contact between Koldo, Pakito and Goiherri, Yoyes joined ETA at the beginning of the 1972-73 academic year, [136] together with several other members of the *cuadrilla*. Her recruitment to the group took place amid the momentous events sweeping the Basque Country in the late 1960s and early 1970s. In the summer of 1968 ETA carried out its first assassination — that of a popularly hated police inspector and torturer in Gipuzkoa named Meliton Manzanas. The assassination provoked a swift response on the part of the Spanish government as thousands of Basques were jailed, tortured and sentenced to several years in prison. According to Robert P. Clark it was during this time — the moment that Yoyes first entertained thoughts about joining ETA — that, "the entire Basque Country lived under a state of siege for many months." [137] The period culminated in the infamous Burgos trial of 1970 when fifteen ETA suspects faced a military court for involvement in the assassination of Manzanas. All except one of the accused were subsequently found guilty and six were sentenced to death. However Franco, bowing to both domestic and international pressure through 1971, later commuted all of the death sentences to thirty-year prison sentences. [138]

From about the middle of 1972 onwards, coinciding with the aftermath of a strong international reaction against the Burgos proceedings and a surge of domestic support from many Basques in favor of an armed response to the dictator-

---

136   Koldo, cited in Garmendia Lasa *et al, Desde su ventana*, p. 33.

137   Robert P. Clark, *Negotiating with ETA: Obstacles to Peace in the Basque Country, 1975-1988* (Reno and Las Vegas: University of Nevada Press, 1990), p. 9.

138   Clark, *The Basque Insurgents*, pp. 54—56.

ship, there was a noticeable rise in ETAs activities. This in turn provoked a severe government crackdown. It subsequently proved to be the critical historical moment when the social base of the organization was radically transformed.

From its inception in 1959 ETA had been led by intellectuals and petty bourgeois students, mainly from the province of Bizkaia. By the early 1970s the majority of the group's new militants came from Gipuzkoa. In the main they were young Basque-speakers from small rural towns affected by the recent immigration of non-Basque speaking people, and an official state policy of linguistic and cultural repression. [139]

From the early 1970s onwards it was from the *Goierri,* the birthplace of Yoyes, that ETA recruited most of its support and activists. "An unusual combination," observes Clark of the region, "of geography [which sheltered the Basque language and culture from its neighbors], [relatively late] industrial development, and culture has produced what may be a unique mixture of the economic aspects of industrial capitalism and the ethnic and cultural aspects of preindustrial society." [140] In his view, the rapid social and economic upheavals experienced by the towns and villages of the *Goierri* provoked a degree of dislocation and stress which, when coupled with official state repression and cultural stigmatization, only compounded a widespread feeling (among the region's Basque-speaking youth) of resentment and hostility. "ETA," contends Clark, "is a product of the Goierri." [141] For Francisco Letamendía Belzunce, the nucleus of ETA from the early 1970s onwards was increasingly comprised of young working-class Basque-speaking youths of peasant origin who felt a sense of displace-

139   Francisco Letamendía Belzunce [Ortzi, pseud.], *Historia del nacionalismo vasco y de E.T.A.,* vol. 1, *E.T.A. en el Franquismo (1951— 1976)* (Donostia-San Sebastián: R&B Ediciones, 1994), pp. 371-74.

140   Clark, *The Basque Insurgents,* p. 200.

141   Ibid., p. 203.

ment or exile within their own communities. [142] It might well be a description of Yoyes herself; the daughter of a union between the two worlds — Spanish/Basque, immigrant/ native, industrial/rural.

The Spanish police first formally identified Yoyes as a member of ETA after she had taken part in the robbery of a duplicator from the college La Salle de Zumárraga in Donostia in August 1973. According to police reports, she may also have participated, two months later, in a failed attempt to bomb a *Guardia Civil* bus in Amara, a suburb of the Gipuzkoan capital. [143] In fear for her safety amid the reprisals taking place throughout the Spanish Basque Country in the early 1970s, she fled on December 15, 1973, to *Iparralde* (the northern Basque Country) in France.

She would live for the next six years in Baiona (Bayonne), during which time she worked as a secretary for the Basque cultural magazine, *Enbata*. At the same time she also gradually assumed more organizational responsibility within ETA. For example, she began to coordinate the ETA commandos of Bilbo (Bilbao) as well as the diverse *taldeak* (groups or sectors) of ETA in the province of Gipuzkoa. Yoyes was emerging as an increasingly enigmatic figure within the organization, teaching classes, for example, in social and political theory and action to exiled ETA members, as well as coordinating much of the group's activities, [144] and involving herself in several feminist groups in Baiona. In 1975 she also met her future husband, Juanjo Dorronsoro, a teacher in Donostia, and Dorronsoro would subsequently visit her frequently in *Iparralde.*

142   Letamendía Belzunce, *Historia del nacionalismo vasco*, vol. 1, *E.T.A. en el Franquismo*, pp. 374—75.

143   José Díaz Herrera and Miguel Angel Liso, "El retorno de la etarra," *Cambio 16* (November 4, 1985), p. 21; the incident is also commented on in some detail by Koldo in Garmendia Lasa *et al, Desde su ventana*, p. 36.

144   Ibid.

Furthermore, exile in the French state did not imply the end of a more active militancy in ETA. Indeed she crossed the border clandestinely on more than one occasion during this period of her life. [145] For example, one ETA member recalled an *ekintza* (action) that he took part in with Yoyes while Spain was still under Franco's rule, and the role that she played in his initiation:

> To get to the government trade union building I was wearing an anorak, the sort that had a pocket here, so that in there I was carrying a live explosive. The explosive was already wired up. We headed for the government building. It was surrounded by the police. But we looked like an ordinary couple, like sweethearts with our arms around each other. We got near the window of the building, lent against the wall, and, still embracing, I managed to get hold of the explosive and leave it on the window. We then headed off and went into a bar. I was nervous but Yoyes was very calm. And while in the bar we heard the explosion five or ten minutes later. [146]

During Yoyes' exile in *Iparralde* ETA underwent a dramatic transformation in 1974. Divisions within the organization (already apparent in the late 1960s with the shift of its social base from urban Bizkaia to rural Gipuzkoa) were compounded that year as the group split into two distinct sections: the *político-militar* faction or ETA (pm), which favored the creation of a mass organization and was equally committed to the class as well as the national struggle; and the more intransigent and nationally-oriented *militar* faction or ETA (m) which persisted with the clandestine armed struggle of its small cells.

---

145   For example she spent time in both Iruñea (Pamplona) and Bilbo, clandestinely organizing ETA activity. See Garmendia Lasa *et al, Desde su ventana,* pp. 40-42.

146   "Esmith" (sic) in "States of Terror" (BBC Television).

While many, such as Goiherri, sided with ETA (pm), the exiled Yoyes remained close to the chief leader of ETA (m), José Miguel Beñarán Ordeñana or "Argala," for whom she maintained an intense admiration, and from 1974 onwards rose swiftly up the ranks within the more hard line faction. By 1977, at the age of twenty-three, she came to occupy a central position in the hierarchy of ETA (m) as the "right-hand woman" of Argala [147] and, together with Domingo Iturbe Abasolo or "Txomin," the head of the organization's political office. [148]

In 1975 General Franco died after nearly forty years in control of Spain. For the next two years the country edged towards a more democratic political system. After the June 1977 general elections in the Spanish state, the first since the death of Franco, a debate emerged among the various representatives of Basque nationalism as to what should be their response to the changes underway in post-Francoist Spain. A meeting was subsequently held that year in Ziburu (Ciboure) in *Iparralde* among the different factions of Basque nationalism. ETA (m)'s delegates were Argala, Txomin, Javier Aya Zulaika or "Trepa" and Yoyes. According to a participant at this meeting, Yoyes "was the hardest of all. She insisted on the principle that if there were no general amnesty for all ETA prisoners, they should destroy the elections." [149]

That same summer of 1977, Argala, Txornin and Yoyes (together with two other members) formed part of the team created by ETA (m) to negotiate the incorporation of another Basque nationalist group, *Bereziak*. Created in January 1975 for the purpose of taking part in high-risk *ekintzak,* the **berezt** commandos had been expelled from ETA (pm) in 1977 after

147   Alcedo Moneo, *Militar en ETA*, p. 130.

148   Clark, *Negotiating with ETA*, p. 163; Diaz Herrera and Liso, "El retorno," p. 21.

149   Díaz Herrera and Liso, "El retorno," p. 22.

their kidnapping and assassination of the Basque industrialist, Javier Ibarra. [150] Once again, according to witnesses of this meeting, it was Yoyes who imposed the hardest conditions on those members of *Bereziak* wanting to join ETA(m). [151]

In a BBC Television documentary about ETA screened originally in 1979, which secretly interviewed several members of the organization, Yoyes appeared as the most dynamic, assured and hard line of the various interviewees. In contemplating the use of political violence, for example, her convictions were clear: "Either we fight or we die anyway. If we die fighting, well, that's the way it goes. But if we don't fight the Basques will certainly perish." [152] Goiherri, her friend and colleague from Ordizia, later recalled that for him Yoyes was "always a brave and dedicated woman. She worried a lot about others and endeavored to ascertain that the actions which had to be taken were just and ethical. We were surprised when she went with ETA *militar* [after the split between ETA (m) and ETA (pm) in 1974]." [153]

And yet at the end of 1977 and the beginning of 1978, at the very moment that Yoyes represented the most dedicated conviction to the armed struggle within ETA, she also began to suffer a crisis of conscience in that same cause. "The explosive mixture," argues Clark about this period, "of a new and more radicalized element within ETA [the *Bereziak* group] plus the growing frustration, unrest, and discontent among Basques generally... would shortly drive the level of violence to new heights." [154] And the turn of events through 1978 and 1979 transformed Yoyes' previously solid conviction in the

---

150   Clark, *The Basque Insurgents,* pp. 83, 88-103.

151   Díaz Herrera and Liso, "El retorno," p. 22.

152   "Panorama" (BBC Television, 1979), cited in "States of Terror" (BBC Television).

153   Cited in Diaz Herrera and Liso, "El retorno," p. 22.

154   Clark, *The Basque Insurgents,* p. 103.

hardest of strategies with regard to the armed struggle into a deepening crisis.

If indeed the period between the end of 1977 and late 1979 marks "a turning point in the history of ETA," [155] then Yoyes' decision to leave the organization must be considered, retrospectively, as crucial to understanding this shift. According to Pedro Ibarra Güell, ETA, which had experienced a low point in its fortunes at the beginning of 1978, recovered during the rest of the year and through 1979 because of two events: the creation in April 1978 of Herri Batasuna (HB), a political coalition party sympathetic to radical Basque nationalism; and the democratic rejection of the new Spanish Constitution by the Basque electorate in December 1978. [156] These events produced a period of intense activity on the part of ETA, together with the appearance of a host of right-wing Spanish anti-terrorist assassination squads that specifically targeted members of ETA. [157]

The major influence on Yoyes' political shift of conviction was, however, personal: the death of her friend and mentor, Argala. In December 1978 Argala was killed in Donibane Lohitzune (St. Jean de Luz) when an explosive charge was set off while starting his car. [158] The incident was subsequently attributed to the *Batallón Vasco Español* (Spanish Basque Battalion), a right-wing group with alleged links to the Spanish police. [159] Coinciding with this intensive period of ETA activity, the private effect of Argala's death was telling. Leta-

---

155   Ibid.

156   Pedro Ibarra Güell, *Ta evolución estratégica de ETA. (De la « guerra revolucionaria » (1963) a la negotiación (1987))* (Donostia: Kriselu, 1987), p. 124.

157   Clark, *The Basque Insurgents,* p. 110.

158   Clark, *The Basque Insurgents,* p. 110; John Sullivan, *ETA and Basque Nationalism: The Fight for Euskadi, 1890-1986* (London and New York: Routledge, 1988), p. 224.

159   Sullivan, *ETA and Basque Nationalism,* p. 224; Díaz Herrera and Liso, "El retorno," p. 22.

188 | WRITINGS IN HONOR OF BASQUE WOMEN

mendia Belzunce characterizes this effect as culminating in "a strong personal crisis," [160] which would ultimately convince her to distance herself from the even more hard line strategy being employed by ETA during this time.

Throughout 1979 Yoyes, who had actually replaced her deceased friend and comrade Argala in the military hierarchy of ETA (m), struggled with this personal crisis over the continued merits of the armed struggle. It would seem as if her anxiety revolved around the issue of to what extent such a struggle should be pursued. The conclusion she reportedly drew was that a degree, at least, of conciliation was necessary to foment a lasting solution to the Basque struggle. [161] Yet any hint of compromise amid the tense situation of the late 1970s was impossible to pursue. She thus came to a definitive decision: a complete break from both ETA and the Basque Country. "I left [ETA] in 1979," she later recalled, "anticipating that the social aspect of the movement, its progressive dimension, would disappear, [only] aiding a militarism based exclusively on a mythical and darker nationalism." [162] At the time of her decision she was, together with Txomin, without question *the* leader of ETA. [163]

Exile 1980–1985

In January 1980 she boarded a train in Dax station, just to the north of *Iparralde* (so as to avoid attention) and, without telling even her closest friends where she was going, she left the Basque Country. [164] Her final destination would be Mexico

160   Letamendía Belzunce, *Historia del nacionalismo vasco*, vol. 3, *E.T.A. y el gobierno del PSOE (1982-1992)*, p. 109.

161   James E. Jacob, *Hills of Conflict: Basque Nationalism in France* (Reno, Las Vegas and London: University of Nevada Press, 1994), pp. 316-17.

162   Yoyes, "Fragmentos," p. 68.

163   Díaz Herrera and Liso, "El retorno," p. 22.

164   Etcheverry, "Mon amie Yoyes," p. 27.

and there, Yoyes began a new life as a student, teacher, wife and mother. She quickly settled in Mexico City, became "Nekane" (the Basque for Dolores) to her friends, and while working part-time at the Mexico City headquarters of the United Nations, studied for a degree in Sociology at the *Universidad Autónoma*. Finishing among the best students of her class five years later, she accepted a teaching position at the same university and, to all intents and purposes, had seemingly settled into a new life in Mexico.

At the time the Spanish police believed that she had gone to Mexico in an official capacity; in other words to oversee ETA operations and form part of a separate exiled leadership, should events in the French state change and prove difficult for ETA (m) to maintain its organizational infrastructure in *Iparralde*. "Nothing further from the truth," recalled her husband Juanjo Dorronsoro, "in Mexico she was never a political refugee. On her identity card she put 'student'." [165] It remained difficult, however, to convince the official authorities of this change. In the summer of 1982 Colonel Pacheco, one of the leading figures of Mexico's *Servicios de Prevención de la Delincuentia*, came to Madrid with a plan to assassinate several Basque exiles in Mexico, among them Yoyes. Pacheco hoped to convince one of the various clandestine right-wing Spanish organizations dedicated to assassinating radical Basque nationalists of his idea, but was ultimately unsuccessful in his goal. [166]

Back in Mexico, and free from the intense nature of involvement in the cause of radical Basque nationalism, Yoyes had, by the early 1980s, apparently settled into a relatively stable domestic and professional lifestyle, marked especially by marriage to long-time companion Juanjo Dorronsoro, who managed to obtain leave from his teaching position and live in

---

165   Cited in Díaz Herrera and Liso, "El retorno," p. 23.

166   Díaz Herrera and Liso, "El retorno," p. 23.

Mexico between 1981 and 1983, and the birth of their son, Akaitz, in November 1982. Yet, after Juanjo had to return to the Basque Country, and in what would be another major personal crisis with wider political ramifications, she increasingly believed that her recently born son should have the opportunity to grow up with his father. In December 1984, convinced that she should attempt a move back to Europe, she spent a month in the French capital, Paris. While in France she took the opportunity to visit Miarritze (Biarritz), meeting the closest of her old friends from her first exile in *Iparralde,* though she was not able to meet some ex-ETA colleagues (Txomin among them) as she had hoped.

On her return to Mexico in 1985, though she had not been able to talk with ETA about its position, she remained convinced in her decision to move back to Europe. In June that same year she initially re-located to Paris where she began to take French classes with a view to undertaking a doctorate in Sociology. However, she remained consumed by the idea of returning to *Hegoalde* (the Southern Basque Country), the land of her birth that she had not seen for a decade.

In August 1985 she arranged a clandestine meeting with her old comrade Txomin in Miarritze. By the mid 1980s Txomin (Domingo Iturbide Abasolo) was one of Europe's most wanted fugitives, hunted at the same time by not only the official forces of the Spanish and French states, but also by the officially, though secretly, sanctioned Spanish death squads, GAL. Between late 1983 and mid 1987 the GAL *(Grupos Antiterroristas de Liberación* or Antiterrorist Liberation Groups) were responsible for twenty-eight killings of suspected radical Basque nationalist sympathizers. [167] It subsequently emerged that both the Spanish Socialist Party (PSOE), the governing party at the time, and the Security Forces were implicated in

---

167   See Clark, *Negotiating with ETA,* pp. 64-68; Jacob, *Hills of Conflict,* pp. 293-303.

organizing GAL. After Yoyes' flight from the organization Txornin had assumed sole leadership of ETA.[168]

At the meeting he promised, for his part at least, that there would be no reprisals against her if she were to accept the Spanish government amnesty and return to *Hegoalde,* on the one condition that she should abstain from speaking in favor of the Spanish government offer of political "reinsertion" or amnesty, nor become a tool of the authorities in their desire to promote this policy.[169] However, as Txornin himself cautioned, the organization was itself divided and he could not speak for the myriad of cells and active groups within ETA. In his opinion it would have been better to remain in Paris.[170]

On her return to Paris, and through September 1985, she worked (through an intermediary) on the possibility of returning to the Spanish state under the 1977 government amnesty. With the prospect of the potential return of an ex-ETA hierarchy leader, the Spanish Ministry of the Interior could not refuse her request. It would be an ideal opportunity to make a political statement about the official government policy of reinsertion. Her decision to return, in her own words, was due to "the pain of being far from loved ones."[171] It would seem, then, that once again this was a choice made less on political principle and more for personal reasons:

> On considering that my return could be undertaken in a dignified manner, the same as those of the other thousands of cases of exiles in the world who return to their countries in similar circumstances . . . I decided to end my exile.[172]

168 For a brief biography of Txomin see Clark, *The Basque Insurgents,* pp. 212—13.

169 Letamendía Belzunce, *Historia del nacionalismo vasco,* vol. 3, *E.TA.J el gobierno del PSOE (1982-1992),* p. 109; Sullivan, *ETA and Basque Nationalism,* p. 264.

170 Garmendia Lasa *et al, Desde su ventana,* pp. 182-83.

171 Yoyes, "Fragmentos," p. 69.

172 Ibid., p. 70.

"I exist," she recalled in her still convincingly existential way, "I have a son, I want to live."[173]

Return 1985–1986

In October 1985 Yoyes crossed the border into *Hegoalde*. "I came on October 11 to San Sebastián," she recorded at the time. "Too familiar! Too strange . . . I'm happy to be with A[kaitz] and J[uanjo]."[174] Throughout 1986 Yoyes settled in Donostia as best she could. However, the Spanish government and media were increasingly using her return in a highly public propaganda campaign against ETA. "It's as if they had made an agreement to kill me," she lamented. "On the front cover of *Cambio 16 (A* Spanish political magazine) they have put a 'robotic' photo of me and a headline that says 'The Return of the *Etarra'* [ETA member]." [175] In its editorial, for example, *Cambio 16* asserted that, "if Yoyes can peacefully return to a society of peaceful [human] beings . . . [then] why are her comrades, in prison or in exile, going to continue the useless struggle? That is the bomb of peace which threatens the narrow universe of the *etarra* of death." [176]

According to at least one observer her return was specifically and very publicly used by the Spanish authorities to re-inforce an offer of amnesty to 150 known ETA exiles. This in return provoked a published response from the exiles, in which they denounced her return to *Hegoalde* and the manner in which, according to press reports, it had been principally a personal decision. Yoyes' silence on the issue might confirm the agreement she had struck with Txornin prior to her re-

---

173 From Marie-France Etchegoin and Serge Raffy, "ETA: La saga des tueurs fantômes," in *Ee Nouvel Observateur* (April 26-May 2, 1990), p. 131, cited in Jacob, *Hills of Conflict*, p. 317.

174 Yoyes, "Fragmentos," p. 65.

175 Ibid.

176 Juan Tomás de Salas, "Editorial," in *Cambio 16*, no. 727 (November 4, 1985), p. 3.

turn. [177] Only a week into this return it was clear that an image of Yoyes had already been created to sustain a rhetorical or discursive struggle between the Spanish government and ETA. And in great part, argues Letamendía Belzunce, this suggests that, "Yoyes was completely distanced from this media maneuver." [178]

The situation was far from comfortable for either Yoyes or her family. In Ordizia that same October placards appeared on the walls of the town denouncing her as a traitor and informer although they were quickly removed. Perhaps this was due to the fact that her decision to return had, indeed, been a personal one. However the fact that several of her own family still led active political lives as members and militants of *Herri Batasuna* (HB), the radical Basque nationalist political party (including one who was even a city councilman for Ordizia) must have also been decisive in the initial rejection of this campaign. [179]

During those first few months she felt the police were watching her every move. While her husband Juanjo continued to teach in the *ikastola* (Basque language school), Liceo Santo Tomás, she sought out several friends from her youth and visited her family in Ordizia frequently, while looking for work. She spoke to her friends of her love for books, in particular the work of de Beauvoir and Virginia Woolf, and privately enjoyed entering into political debate. But above all she seems, at this time, to have found stability in her own domestic family, with Juanjo and Akaitz. [180] She was, however, also discovering a "different" Basque Country to the one she had left in 1973, for post-Franco Basque society had changed dramatically.

177 Letamendía Belzunce, *Historia del nacionalismo vasco*, vol. 3, *E.T.A. y el gobierno del PSOE (1982-1992)*, pp. 109-10.

178 Ibid., p. 109.

179 Ibid., p. 110.

180 Etcheverry, "Mon amie Yoyes," p. 29.

Domestic happiness could not, however, remove the fear of reprisal. In July 1986 a French government crackdown (as a response to GAL activity in France) resulted in the handing over of a stream of Basque political refugees. That same month Txomin was also arrested in France and deported to Gabon in Africa, leaving a power vacuum within the ETA hierarchy and allowing more hard line leaders to assume control in his absence. [181] Among the new leadership was Pakito, a friend of Yoyes from her *cuadrilla* in Ordizia. ETA's military chief since January 1985, he was now known by the *nom de guerre*, "Artapalo." After Txomin's arrest, Artapalo would become the overall leader of ETA. [182]

Throughout 1986 graffiti and placards on the walls of Ordizia calling Yoyes a "traitor" and "informer" appeared once more. Even with this in mind, on September 9 that same year she and Akaitz went to Ordizia to see the famous Basque fair of the town, which traditionally celebrated the produce of this rural center. The following day she took the opportunity to meet with old friends, among them (briefly) Koldo from her *cuadrilla*. Later on that day, while walking in the main square of the town, a man approached her. According to later police reports,

> the witness approached Yoyes and asked her: "Are you Yoyes?" She asked him who he was, to which he replied: "I am from ETA and I have come to execute you." Immediately he fired two shots from his pistol into her breast and when she fell to the ground he finished her off with another shot to the head. [183]

---

181   Clark, *Negotiating with ETA*, p. 163; Jacob, *Hills of Conflict*, p. 317; Sullivan, *ETA and Basque Nationalism*, p. 262.

182   Clark, *Negotiating with ETA*, p. 169; Jacob, *Hills of Conflict*, p. 317.

183   Cited in "States of Terror" (BBC Television).

Allegedly, on the orders of Artapalo, a member of the *Goiherri-kosta* commando of ETA, José Antonio López Ruiz ("Kubati"), carried out the assassination. It took place just a few days after Txomin's arrival in Algeria from Gabon, demonstrating "the degree to which Iturbe's control over the organization might be slipping." [184]

In April 1987 an HB representative from Nafarroa, Inaki Aldekoa, commenting on the death of Yoyes, observed that, "an army cannot allow deviations and especially from one of its generals." [185] A month later, in an interview ceded to a French journal, ETA members themselves explained their decision:

> Yoyes had important responsibilities among us. After a period of personal and ideological degradation, she had chosen the worst of paths: repentance, treason, collaboration with the enemy. The "repentant" are used to legitimate the repression. As a consequence, they are in the service of the enemy. [186]

Similarly, in an interview with leaders of ETA that appeared in the December 1988 edition of the magazine *Diario 16,* they were asked how they could have sanctioned the assassination of someone who shared their beliefs. They responded that, "she shared them up until a certain time. From that moment on, the senior and qualified militant of the organization that she was, Yoyes decided to take sides against the National Liberation Movement." [187]

---

184   Clark, *Negotiating with ETA,* p. 179.

185   Cited in Letamendía Belzunce, *Historia del nacionalismo vasco,* vol. 3, *E.TA.y el gobierno del PSOE (1982-1992),* p. 112.

186   Interview with Armando Puente, "Trois membres de l'ETA parlent," in *Le Point* (May 25, 1987), p. 86, cited in Jacob, *Hills of Conflict,* p. 317.

187   Original interview in *Diario 16* (December 1988), cited in Luis Nuñez *et al, Euskadi eta Askatasuna. Euskal Herria j la Libertad,* vol. 7, *La ofensiva institucional 1985-1988* (Tafalla: Txalaparta, 1993), p. 309; the

Friends from her youth in Ordizia, although unrepentant about their involvement in ETA, reacted with shock. "That day," recalled Koldo, "I was watching a game of *pelota* because it was the village *fiesta*. I was very upset. I felt a great pain ... a great pain." Similarly, Goiherri observed that, "on a personal level I was upset because I knew her ... I didn't think they would go that far." [188] Several hundred former members of ETA subsequently attended her funeral. [189]

For Alcedo Moneo her execution was the extermination of a category, that of "military traitor." In this sense she was perceived by ETA to have been a traitor to her responsibilities to such an extent that she hurt the image of the organization itself. [190] Letamendía Belzunce views her execution as a kind of ritual sacrifice, so as to maintain the resolve of, and prevent any division among, the exiled community of Basque political refugees. [191] With the assassination of Yoyes, the policy of reinsertion suffered a tremendous blow and, in the opinion of some commentators, forced the Spanish government into the still existent policy of dispersion of Basque political prisoners in jails outside the Basque Country, after 1987. [192] This is a policy which subsequently provoked one of the most important political demands of Basque nationalism in the 1990s, namely the return of political prisoners to the Basque Country under the tenets of UN-sanctioned international law; a

---

same interview is translated in "History and Historical Documents about the Basque Armed Organization Euskadi ta Askatasuna (ETA): Interview with the Leadership of ETA Military" (Source: Euskadi Information, Bulletin of Ekin, February 1990). At http://www.contrast.org/mirrors/ehj/html/etaintlb.html.

188   "States of Terror" (BBC Television).

189   Jacob, *Hills of Conflict,* p. 317.

190   Alcedo Moneo, *Militar en ETA,* p. 130.

191   Letamendía Belzunce, *Historia del nacionalismo vasco,* vol. 3, *E.T.A.j el gobierno del PSOE (1982-1992),* p. 110.

192   Nuñez *et al, Euskadi eta Askatasuna,* vol. 7, *La ofensiva institucional,* pp. 76-78.

demand that, as recently as January 1999, drew a hundred thousand people to the streets of Bilbo (Bilbao) to protest the continuation of the dispersion policy.

Conclusion

"Great errors," observes Joseba Zulaika, "not arbitrary murders, are the stuff of tragedy." [193] This, I think, explains in great part the tragedy of Yoyes. Within the dramatic narrative of Basque political violence she stands out as a tragic figure, a tragic heroine even, who, for some, erroneously fell from purity into vice. For others the error was committed in her assassination. Yoyes' story thus reveals the tragedy of sacrifice and loss that has engulfed Basque political culture in recent memory.

Part of the tragedy of Yoyes lies also, I suspect, in the timing of her return to the Basque Country, coinciding as it did with the wave of assassinations carried out by GAL. She was, as a consequence, and during the brief, intense period between 1985 and 1986, guilty by association; an association with the official Spanish government authorities that were, at the same time, sponsoring both a public policy of social reinsertion and a private policy of death squads. [194]

It would seem that Yoyes, as a woman involved in ETA, was always going to be plagued by an associative role. According to Aretxaga, women do have important roles to play within the discourse of radical Basque nationalism but these roles are usually dependent on men. So where men are the *gudariak* (warriors) and initiators of the radical discourse, women are

---

193   Joseba Zulaika, *Basque Violence: Metaphor and Sacrament* (Reno and Las Vegas: University of Nevada Press, 1988), p. 91.

194   Cf. Letamendía Belzunce, *Historia del nacionalismo vasco,* vol. 3, *E.TA.y el gobierno del PSOE (1982-1992),* p. 111.

the strong and supportive wives and mothers. [195] In many ways the life and death of Yoyes, and its subsequent reduction within studies of Basque political violence, has also been reduced to an associative meaning. Mention Yoyes and commentators speak of what her death *meant,* for Basque nationalism or for changes in Spanish government policy towards the Basque Country. What seems to be most often lost is what she actually *did,* what her actions *meant* for Basque nationalism itself. And this is, perhaps, the most tragic aspect of all.

---

195   Begoña Aretxaga, *Eos funerales en el nacionalismo radical vasco* (n.p.: Baroja, 1988), p. 101.

Language, Love, and Lyricism: Basque Women Writers Urretabizkaia, Mintegi, and Oñederra

Linda White

The relationship between gender and writing, coupled with the state of perceived female gender identity in Spain, combine to create a field ripe for interpretation and comparison through the fiction of three of the culture's most prominent women writers. Works written in a minority language are often judged by the stylistic imperatives of more mature majority literatures. By viewing three Basque women writers, Arantxa Urretabizkaia, Laura Mintegi, and Lourdes Oñederra, in the light of discussions on gender, minority literature, and nationalism, we can observe changes in the status of women and in the state of literature created by them within Basque society.

Here I examine three Basque women together with the outside influences and inside pressures that condition their fiction. The situation of feminism in Spain results in a paradox for working women in general, [196] including those who write in Basque. As a feminist critic coming to Basque litera-

---

196   See Cristina Alberdi, "Estrategias para conseguir la igualdad," in Edurne Uriarte and Arantxa Elizondo, eds. *Mujeres en política: Andlisis y practica* (Barcelona: Ariel, 1997), pp. 303-311 and Maria Antonia Garcia de Leon, "Mujeres en politica: El caso paradójico de una élite dominada y discriminada," in Rita Radl Philipp and María Carmen García Negro, eds. *As mulleres e os cambios socials e económicos* (Santiago de Compostela: Universidade de Santiago de Compostela, 1995), pp. 15-32.

ture from a North American framework, I am unable to avoid seeking out the feminist aspect in these women's writings. The relationship between gender and writing as described by Heilbrun and Schulz, [197] and the state of perceived female gender identity in Spain examined by Radl Philipp, [198] combine to create a field ripe for interpretation and comparison, allowing the reader to view a conflicted reality within Basque society through the fiction of three of the culture's most prominent women writers.

Of the literature surrounding minority language issues, JanMohamed and Lloyd express the need for a theory of minority discourse across international literary boundaries, [199] while Camartin, Green, Leal, and Mar-Molinero discuss limitations, status, and literary criticism within specific language frames. [200] These general theories indicate that works writ-

197   Carolyn G. Heilbrun, *Writing a Woman's Life* (New York: Ballantine, 1988); Muriel Schulz, "Minority Writers: The Struggle for Authenticity and Authority," in Cheris Kramrae, Muriel Schulz, and William M. O'Barr, eds. *Language and Power* (Beverly Hills: Sage, 1984), pp. 206-217.

198   Rita Radl Philipp, "La nueva identidad del género femenino en los debates de la televisión," in Radl Philipp and Garcia Negro, eds. *As mulleres*, pp. 77—96.

199   Abdul R. JanMohamed and David Lloyd, "Toward a Theory of Minority Discourse: What Is To Be Done?" in Abdul R. JanMohamed and David Lloyd, eds. *The Nature and Context of Minority Discourse* (New York and Oxford: Oxford University Press, 1990).

200   Iso Camartin, "Romanche, a Minor Literature: Limitations and Perspectives," in John L. Flood, ed. *Modern Swiss Literature: Unity and Diversity* (New York: St. Martin's, 1985), John N. Green, "Language Status and Political Aspirations: The Case of Northern Spain," in M. Mair Parry, Winifred V. Davies, and Rosalind A. M. Temple, eds. *The Changing Voices of Europe: Social and Political Changes and Their Linguistic Repercussions, Past, Present and Future* (Cardiff, Wales: University of Wales Press, Modern Humanities Research Association, 1994), pp. 155-172, Luis Leal, "Literary Criticism and Minority Literatures: The Case of the Chicano Writer," *Confluencia*, vol. 1, no. 2 (1986), pp. 4—9, and Clare Mar-Molinero, "The Politics of Language: Spain's Minority Languages," in Helen Graham and Jo Labanyi, eds. *Spanish Cultural Studies: An Introduction: The Struggle for Modernity* (Oxford and New York: Oxford University Press, 1995), pp. 336-42.

ten in a minority language are often judged by the stylistic imperatives of more mature majority literatures. Dorian, for example, acknowledges the pressures felt by speakers of a minority language to move toward the majority tongue:

> It's fairly common for a language to become so exclusively associated with low-prestige people and their socially disfavored identities that its own potential speakers prefer to distance themselves from it and adopt some other language. Parents in these circumstances will make a conscious or unconscious decision not to transmit the ancestral language to their children, and yet another language will be lost. [201]

In the case of modern Basque society outside forces, specifically the Spanish and French states, traditionally stigmatized *Euskara* (Basque), and for centuries most Basque-speakers felt that their language was solely for use in the home and family. As a consequence all official documents, for example, were recorded in Spanish or French. This meant that the earliest producers of literature in Euskara spent considerable time and energy celebrating its glory and beauty at the expense of literary creation. This trend continued into the twentieth century, when supporters of the language also began taking steps to maintain Euskara in the face of overwhelming pressures from the majority languages.

On the French side of the border Euskara was not persecuted but rather ignored. This gross marginalization was reinforced by a school system that employed French and left no room for literacy in, or maintenance of, minority tongues. Basque author Itxaro Borda spoke only Euskara until she started school. However, by her third year of elementary school

---

201   Nancy C. Dorian, "Western Language Ideologies and Small-language Prospects," in L. A. Genoble and L. J. Whaley, eds. *Endangered Languages: Language Loss and Community Response* (Cambridge: Cambridge University Press, 1998), p. 3.

she was fluent in French and rapidly losing her Basque-language skills. [202] On the Spanish side, the oppressive Franco years (1939 – 75) made it difficult in the extreme for Basque speakers to maintain their language. Franco's regime imposed a strident monolingualism throughout Spain, forbidding publication and schooling in, and general usage of, the principal minority tongues: Euskara, Gallego, and Catalán. Indeed, many families lost Euskara completely before Franco died in 1975, because for safety's sake it was politically expedient to distance oneself from the language. Basque parents were, then, forced to make the wrenching decision, on behalf of their children, of whether to teach them Euskara or not. [203]

As a consequence, the nationalist movement has been an important factor in the Basque case, both as a motivator for supporting Euskara and as a stimulus for writing in the language. Expressing literature in Euskara has been an acceptable nationalist activity for women, whereas social pressures to remain within the domestic or private sphere kept most from more public displays of support. In fact, both women's identity and their role in Franco's Spain were shaped through the use of language that defined them as "indoor heroines." [204] While women are generally missing from na-

---

202 Personal interview with the author. Borda made it a point to become very involved in her daughter's school, one of the few *ikastolak* (schools that instruct via Euskara) in France.

203 This is what happened in the vast majority of Basque-American homes throughout North and South America. Although Spain's laws regarding the banning of minority languages could not touch emigrants and exiles, many Basque-speaking parents living abroad felt that their offspring needed to master the majority language of their new home. In the U.S. and Canada, the children were encouraged to speak English. In Latin America they were urged to use Spanish. These were the languages that would benefit new Americans.

204 Mercedes Carbayo-Abengózar, "Shaping Women: National Identity Through the Use of Language in Franco's Spain," *Nations and Nationalism* vol. 7, no. 1 (2001), pp. 75—92.

tionalist discussions, [205] some scholars address the issue from within the Basque Country [206] and other non-Basque scholars examine the relationships between nationalism, literature, and feminism. [207] From these theoretical perspectives, we might conclude that a Basque literary "style" has evolved which requires hopeful writers to walk a fine line between stylistic lessons learned from majority language reading, and the esthetic requirements that must be met in order to be published in the Basque Country.

An exploration of the work of Urretabizkaia, Mintegi, and Oñederra, taking account of these various discussions, reveals the changes in the status of women and in the state of literature created by them within Basque society. The North American non-native perspective provides a means by which their works can be situated within Basque literature in particular, and within the contexts of feminism and minority literature on both sides of the Atlantic in general.

205   See Cynthia Enloe, *Bananas, Beaches, and Bases: Making Feminist Political Sense of International Politics* (Berkeley and Los Angeles: University of California Press, 1990), Carrie Hamilton, "Remembering the Basque nationalist family," *Journal of Spanish Cultural Studies*, vol. 1, no. 2 (2000), pp. 153-171, Sylvia Walby, "Woman and Nation," in Gopal Balukrishnan, ed. *Mapping the Nation* (London: Verso, 1996), pp. 235-54, and Nira Yuval-Davis, *Gender & Nation* (London, Thousand Oaks, and New Delhi: Sage, 1997).

206   See, for example, Lourdes Méndez, "Identidad de sexo, identidad de género y producción artística: La problemática del reconocimiento social," in Arantza Campos and Lourdes Méndez, eds. *Teoría feminista: identidad, género y política* (San Sebastian: Universidad del País Vasco, 1992), pp. 147-161 and Mercedes Ugalde Solano, *Mujeres y nacionalismo vasco: Genesis y desarrollo de Emakume Abertzale Batza (1906—1936)* (Bilbao: Universidad del País Vasco, 1993).

207   Terry Eagleton, "Nationalism: Irony and Commitment," in Terry Eagleton, Fredric Jameson, and Edward W Said, *Nationalism, Colonialism, and Literature* (Minneapolis: University of Minnesota Press, 1990), pp. 23—42, and Frederic Jameson, "Modernism and Imperialism," in Eagleton, Jameson, and Said, *Nationalism, Colonialism, and Literature*, pp. 43—68.

Arantxa Urretabizkaia's *Zergatik, Panpox?* (Why, Darling?) [208]

This lyrical novella is a stream-of-consciousness narration by a mother whose husband left her six months previously. She has a small child, a son, Antxon, who occupies her every waking thought. In fact, the narrator-mother's thoughts are inextricably woven in and out of the need and desire to care for her child. On the one hand, she is trying to analyze her life: Specifically, why her husband left her and what her nightly dreams mean. More prosaically, she is attentive to the daily realities of being a single mother. For example, Antxon is coughing in the night or she simply wakes up to listen to his breathing:

> Pitilinaren kontua oraindik zertan zegoen erabaki baino lehen esnatu egin nahiz. Antxonek estula egin du, ez eztarrikoa, sakona baizik. Oraindik ez zaio katarroa erabat sendatu. [209]

> (I woke up before I could decide what the wee-wee story was all about. Antxon coughed, not a throat cough, a deep one. He was not yet completely over his cold).

Her never-ending list of chores and maternal duties are recited like a litany: less a prayer *to,* but rather a prayer *from,* motherhood. She is very much aware of her mothering role.

---

208   Arantxa Urretavizcaya (often spelled Urretabizkaia to reflect the standardized orthography of Unified Basque) was born in San Sebastián-Donostia, Spain, in 1947. She studied history at university, worked as a journalist for Euskal Telebista, the Basque-language television channel, and for the film industry. She has written young adult fiction, short stories, poetry, non-fiction, translations, novels, and the novella *Zergatik, panpox?* (Why, darling?), her most acclaimed work. See Linda White, *"Emakumeen Hitzak Euskeraz. Basque Women Writers of the Twentieth Century"* Ph.D. Diss., University of Nevada, Reno, 1996, pp. 194-195.

209   Arantxa Urretabizkaia, *Zergatik, panpox?* (Donostia: Erein, 1979), p. 9.

Indeed, she is obsessed by it. Yet mothers everywhere would view this obsession as completely normal: "Ni, bizitza naiz, eta ukitzen dudan guztia bizirik egongo da" (I am life and everything I touch will have life). [210] This phrase, specifically "ni bizitza naiz" (I am life) and others such as "Zu zara, pan-pox, nere munduko lagunik haundiena" (You, darling, are my biggest help in life) are repeated throughout the book as lyrical refrains that tie the constant stream of thought to the maternal center.

Urretabizkaia's *Zergatik, panpox?* was published in 1979, a scant four years after Franco's death. The situation of women in Spain under Franco had been a difficult one. According to Judith Astelarra,

> Official ideology decreed absolute submission of wives to their husbands and exalted the virtues of obedience, purity, and abnegation for women. These principles were quickly transformed into laws that forbade women's work outside the home, abolished divorce, subordinated married women to their husbands in all respects, punished severely female adultery, and discriminated against children born out of wedlock. [211]

Bombarded throughout their lives with this sort of inculturation, it is understandable if women writers in the Basque Country of Spain were slow in advancing their creative efforts to the point of submission to a publisher. In 1979, Urretabizkaia's assertion of "I am life" was a grand statement that transcended the oppressive silence of the Franco years, yet at the same time remained within the culturally proscribed bound-

---

210 Ibid., p. 18.

211 Judith Astelarra, "Women, Political Culture, and Empowerment in Spain," in Francine D'Amico and Peter R. Beckman, eds. *Women in World Politics: An Introduction* (Westport, Conn, and London: Bergin & Garvey, 1995), p. 42.

aries for women, keeping her subject matter centered on the acceptable role of motherhood.

The plot of the book[212] recounts a day in the life of a single mother. From the moment she awakes, we live within her mind as she wakes her child, makes his breakfast, gets them both ready for the day, and takes him to school. She tries not to think about him between the hours of nine and five, but to no avail. He constantly fills her thoughts. At home once again, she feeds him, bathes him, plays with him, tells him a story, and spends the hour or two after he drifts off to sleep rushing through the chores that did not get done during the day. Interwoven with the single-mother theme is the lost-love theme, the agony of self-searching she experiences while trying to understand why her husband, Txema, left her. What if she runs into him at the market? Should she be friendly? Distant? Aloof, but civil? What was it that drove him away? Cellulite? Broad hips? Who was she now that she had no husband?

Melancholy, despair, resignation, and the maternal drive pull the narrator through her day. She feels guilty because she wanted a daughter and had a son. She fears for her future. She fantasizes about Txema's return, but in the end she doesn't really think that he'll come back. And at the end of her day she's not sure she will survive the winter without him. Yet the reader is left in no doubt. She will survive and continue to move from one maternal chore to another, doing what she must to care for her child and make it through the day.

---

212   For much of the twentieth century, Basque fiction was often brief. What would be considered as story-length fiction or a novella within the English-speaking publishing world was often presented as a complete book or novel in Basque literary circles. During the last ten years of the twentieth century, however, the lengths of published narratives increased.

Love

Just as in 1979 Urretabizkaia wrote an entire book about love, so in 1994 Laura Mintegi focused on the same theme in her novel, *Nerea eta biok* (Nerea and I). This was even more the case in her later novel, *Sisifo maite minez* (Sysiphus in love). Similarly, Lourdes Oñederra wrestled with the destruction that love can cause in people's lives in her 1999 novel, *Eta emakumeari sugeak esan zion* (And the snake said to the woman). These are but three examples of works by women in which love is the prominent focus of the novel, although it might appear as though they were writing in a vacuum, separated by their gender from events in the male literary world. For example, a young male author, Ur Apalategi, stated in a 1997 interview that,

> Orain arte, maitasuna ez baita euskal literaturan gai zentrala izan. Saiatu naiz sentimentuei buruzko nobela bat egiten, baina ez eleberri sentimental bat. Aitzitik, pentsatzen dut nahiko garratza dela, eta ironiaz betea; batere ez idealista gainera
>
> (Until now, love has not been the central theme in Basque literature. I have tried to create a novel about feelings, but not a sentimental novel. On the contrary, I think it is rather bitter, and full of humor; what's more, not at all idealistic). [213]

Novels by male authors *have* dealt with the subject matter of love from the male point of view, but the largely male body of critics has avoided discussing these aspects of their works. [214] This might lead us to speculate that commenting

---

213   Cited in Mikel Asurmendi, "Garaia da obrak idazteko filologian pentsatu gabe," *Argia*, no. 1, 626 (May 25, 1997), p. 44.

214   *Leturiaren egunkari ezkutua* (Leturia's secret diary) (1957) by Txillardegi (a pseudonym of José Luis Alvarez Enparantza) is an existentialist love story. Ramón Saizarbitoria's *Egunero hasten delako* (Because it begins every day)

on feelings and emotional issues betrays some machismo of the male critic's spirit. Bearing in mind that Apalategi's comments reveal more about a young writer's awareness of his literary history than anything else, it is still illustrative of the extant tendency in Basque literary circles to exclude works by women from discussions of literature, as if there were two separate fields: women's writings and "real" literature, namely that written by men. [215]

This exclusion of women authors is not unique to Basque literary circles. For example, Baym goes so far as to say that in American literature the woman writer is perceived as the enemy by male critics, and that those critics dominate the theories which in turn control the reading of American literature thereby effectively excluding women from the can-

---

(1969) is the story of a brief love affair that ends in a teenage pregnancy and abortion. Jon Mirande's *Haur besoetakoa* (The godchild) (1970) is the tale of a pedophile's illicit love for his eleven-year-old goddaughter. These three works are lauded as landmarks in Basque literature. However the critics typically discuss the authors' contributions to style and structure, together with their innovations and modernization of the novel in Euskara. Pointedly, they do not talk about the authors' amorous sentiments in general, while specifically ignoring Saizarbitoria's discussion of abortion and Mirande's treatment of pedophilia. Indeed, one critic at the time, Enrike Zabala, went so far as to suggest of Saizarbitoria's book that it lacked depth and that the events in the book were merely anecdotal, even though the subject matter was one of the most difficult of the Franco era, that of abortion. See Enrike Zabala, *Euskal alfabetatzeko literatura* (Lazkao: Pax, 1979), p. 244.

215　In all fairness, it must be said the critics can be equally hard on men and women. For example, in 1981 Joxe Azurmendi said of Xabier Gereño's detective novels that they were in a sense not really literature (meaning literary fiction), although it did appear that Gereno was creating literature of a sort, developing narrative and attracting readers. Later, however, in a back-handed way, Azurmendi concedes that he does not necessarily scorn that sort of literature and that it must have its place. So male critics do lambaste male writers and set them apart from "real" literature, too. Gereño's novels are quite popular with young adults and with those who are learning Euskara as a second language. See Joxe Azurmendi, "Euskal literaturaren orainaz eta geroaz," in *Euskal linguistika eta literatura: Bide berriak* (Bilbao: Deustuko Unibertsitatea, 1981), pp. 405-452.

on. [216] This pattern of exclusion is also evident in Spanish literature. [217]

Language Use

My discussion of language use is based on the literary texts of the three authors under discussion. It differs, for example, from Carbayo-Abengózar's related, but distinct, investigation of the use of language in official discourses to shape what and how women think of themselves (see note 9). Such investigation is beyond the scope of this article. When Bakhtin spoke of heteroglossia in the novel, defining it as "another's speech in another's language" and "double-voiced discourse," [218] he did not have the diglossic situation of the Basque Country in mind, but his words may certainly be applied to the language problem in Basque literature.

From the beginning of the twentieth century and the birth of the Basque novel, [219] Basque writers demonstrated self-consciousness about their minority tongue. Their fictional universes never seemed to function in Euskara alone and

216   Nina Baym, "Melodramas of Beset Manhood: How Theories of American Fiction Exclude Women Authors," in *The New Feminist Criticism: Essays on Women, Literature and Theory* (New York: Pantheon, 1985), pp. 63-69.

217   Janet Pérez, counting the names of women mentioned in various bibliographies, arrives at a figure of 2,000 women writers in Spain between 1401 and 1988. As she herself observes, "if only the top ten percent of these (i.e., two hundred) are worthy of remembering and reading, they comprise a number well in excess of the minimum necessary to establish a feminist canon and tradition." *Contemporary Women Writers of Spain* (Boston: Twayne, 1988), p. 5.
Instead, Spanish literature anthologies may contain as few as two female authors, most likely Santa Teresa and Emilia Pardo Bazán, according to Pérez (Ibid, p. 5).

218   Mikhail Mikhailovich Bakhtin, *The Dialogic Imagination* (Austin: University of Texas Press, 1981), p. 342.

219   Ana María Toledo Lezeta makes an eloquent case for Txornin Agirre as the first novelist in Basque literature. See *Domingo Agirre: euskal elaberriaren sorrera* (Donostia: Bizkaiako Foru Aldundia, 1989).

the reality of life in a diglossic society regularly intruded into the fictions of the authors themselves. This self-consciousness may have been rooted in the awareness that the earliest attempts to produce literature in Euskara had little to do with art or fiction and more to do with apologistic demonstrations of the versatility and usefulness of the language.

In addition, it is difficult to find a book review or critique that does not address the author's use of Euskara. Is the work in Unified Basque or in another dialect? Does the author use too many Spanish borrowings? Or is the text peppered with unintelligible neologisms? These comments seldom advance to a discussion of stylistics, but rather focus on a writer's prowess in Euskara with regard to grammar and vocabulary. The question of one's ability to construct a story, to master the structure of a novel, is seldom broached. This focus on *language,* as opposed to *literary,* proficiency stems from the precarious situation of Euskara as a minority language and the decades-long battle to save it from extinction. When a literature is the means to a pedagogical end, the quality and purpose of fictional narrative is overshadowed by the need to provide a readership with instructive linguistic models.[220]

Since Basque critics give great weight to the use of Euskara in narrative, it must be addressed even when the critic is a non-Basque, an outsider. To avoid the question would be to ignore the priorities of Basques themselves regarding their

---

220   Jesús María Lasagabaster, Linda White and others have commented on the unusual relationship between Euskara and its literature. Lasagabaster expounds on Basque literature as principally a pedagogical tool while White describes the situation as a literature enslaved to the needs of its minority language. See Lasagabaster, "Introduction," in *Contemporary Basque Fiction: An Anthology* (Reno and Las Vegas: University of Nevada Press, 1990), pp. 1-23, and Linda White, "A Literature in Chains: *Literatura kateatuta*" paper delivered at the First International Symposium on Basque Cultural Studies, London Guildhall University, London, UK, June 29-July 2, 2000. Published on the IBS (Institute of Basque Studies) web site. Go to URL <http://ibs.lgu.ac.uk/sympo/page4.html> and click on "Literature in Chains" in Session Three. Link valid as of April, 2003.

own literature. Not only is an author's use of Euskara worthy of mention but the inclusion or exclusion of other languages in the text is also pertinent. Here we return to the self-consciousness of Basque writers who feel they cannot create a believable universe if it does not reflect the diglossic [221] and polyglot reality of life in the Basque Country. [222]

Urretabizkaia used Spanish words occasionally but she "Basquified" them, if we can invent a verb to describe the process. Indeed, she made them so much a part of her own language that when listening to modern Basque one hardly notices them. This happens in other languages, as well. When an American English speaker says "taco" or "tortilla" those words sound completely English (whether spoken or written) because of both pronunciation and extreme familiarity. This is because American English speakers are the majority language group, so they subsume foreign borrowings harmlessly and effortlessly into the language. Basque speakers are, and have been for centuries, the minority language group, and borrowings from Spanish are often a reminder of that status. Thus Urretabizkaia's use of borrowed words reflected the reality of spoken Basque at the close of the 1970s, especially in the context of a new, post-Franco society where Euskara was no longer (officially at least) stigmatized and persecuted.

---

221   According to John N. Green, "the concept of diglossia ...depends crucially on the inequality of status and power relations. In such a framework, a minority language is almost inevitably one that has been subordinated to, or annexed by, a dominant ideology." See "Language Status and Political Aspirations: The Case of Northern Spain," in Mair Parry, Davies and Temple, eds. *The Changing Voices of Europe*, p. 155. This description was especially true in the decades immediately preceding the publication of *Zergatik, panpox?* By the time Oñederra's novel was published in 1999, the situation had improved, but since Euskara has co-official status with Spanish only within the Comunidad Autónoma Vasca or Basque Autonomous Community (comprising three of the seven Basque provinces), we can still accurately describe it as a diglossic situation.

222   By the end of the twentieth century, Basque authors were creating fictional universes entirely in Euskara, or at the very least they had reduced exolinguistic intrusions to a few scattered words.

In order to transport the reader into the narrator's thoughts, Urretabizkaia dispenses with quotation marks. Her comments, and those of her son, are therefore intertwined with her thoughts. Third party dialog, however, is in Spanish, thereby effectively manipulating the Basque reader's diglossic reality to establish intimate identification with the mother and her world. Everyone else is an outsider. In the words of Hélène Cixous,

> language englobes us and inspires us and launches us beyond ourselves, it is ours and we are its, it is our master and our mistress. And even if it seems to be native or national, it happily remains foreign to those who write. Writing consists first of all in hearing language speak itself to our ears, as if it were the first time. [223]

When reading *Zergatik, panpox?* one cannot help but feel that Urretabizkaia was experiencing this inspiration, that she was hearing her language speak to her in a voice all her own, as if for the first time.

Laura Mintegi's *Nerea eta biok* (Nerea and I)

Mintegi's protagonist, a female university professor, communicates with her correspondence student, a female political prisoner, in Euskara. [224] French and Spanish are the languages used to define the outsiders. The legal documents and prison censors all communicate in French, emphasizing their alien quality. The Spanish police speak only Spanish. As

---

223   Hélène Cixous, *The Hélène Cixous Reader*, ed. Susan Sellers (London: Routledge, 1994), p. xix.

224   For a discussion of the portrayal of Mintegi's female political prisoner and a comparison with that of Bernardo Atxaga's female political activist, see White's "Atxaga's *Lone Woman* and Mintegi's *Nerea eta biok*: Two Different Views of the Female Basque Political Prisoner," *Journal of the Society for Basque Studies in America*, vol. XIV (1999), pp. 17-35.

Urretabizkaia did before her, Mintegi uses the point of view
of a single working mother, but this woman is more engaged
with the world around her, reflecting in many ways the societal changes for women that occurred in the fifteen years
between the publication of *Zergatik, panpox?* (1979) and *Nerea
eta biok* (1994). She is also more aware of the Basque political situation, albeit against her will. Author Mintegi, who is
very involved in Basque politics as well as being a university
professor, uses the story to make a point about the effect that
the treatment of political prisoners has on their families. [225]
Her protagonist is forced to confront issues she doesn't want
to think about when she responds to Nerea's letters, and by
the end of the book, her own family becomes one of those
most deeply affected by the problem when her son is arrested
and imprisoned, and she and her daughter are forced to endure the indignities of prison bureaucracy in order to see him.
Thus the fear she experienced vicariously through Nerea's situation becomes an intense emotional reality in her own life,
through her son's eventual captivity.

---

225   A lot of information is available in print and via the Internet about the
plight of Basque political prisoners. An in-depth discussion of the situation
here would take us away from the topic at hand. However, since the novel under discussion centers on a relationship between two women, one of whom
is in prison, the following comments of Juana M. Balmaseda and María José
Carrera seem appropriate:
*Si los varones presos son los olvidados del sistema social, más aún que ellos son las mujeres
presas, y hasta tal punto que si del genero masculino del lenguaje se dice que gramaticalmente
engloba al género masculino y femenino y que así está conceptualizado también desde el punto
de vista social, cuando se habla del genérico presos sólo se piensa en los varones, como si las
mujeres presas no existieran."*
(If male prisoners are the forgotten ones of the social system, female prisoners are even more so, to such an extent that if it is said of the masculine
gender of language that it encompasses both the masculine and the feminine
and that it is conceptualized thus also from the social point of view, when one
speaks of the generic *presos,* one thinks only of the males, as if female prisoners did not exist).
Balmaseda and Carrera also affirm that discrimination against female prisoners extends to "unthinkable extremes." See "Desigualdad/discriminación
de la mujer en los ámbitos penal y penitenciario," *Herria 2000 Eliza,* no. 144
(1996), pp. 46-7, 48.

Mintegi's character, Isabel, and the events that surround her life, demonstrate how women can be affected by nationalism, restricted by the symbolism of tradition (as expressed by the mother's role), bound by the obligation of producing and educating the children of the nation, and shattered both by the violence that disrupts their families and by the laws that create more difficulties for them as they move through their lives at home and at work. These questions are especially pertinent as women involved in the nationalist movement often embrace their role as mothers of the nation.

> But even if the rhetoric of maternity reflects as well as shapes many women's "daily reality," it also tends to hide fundamental gender inequalities .. .Moreover, the privileging of women as mothers masks the important material contributions women have made to nationalist movements above and beyond the call of maternal duty. [226]

Mintegi also addresses the female condition in the novel through lengthy *in absentia* conversations with Nerea about the nature of love and lesbianism. Mintegi's other works demonstrate an evolution of her themes from an early preoccupation with nationalism and politics to a serious investigation of unbridled love, especially in her most recent novel, *Sisifo maite minez* (Sysiphus in love). With regard to stylistic influences from other literatures, while her earlier ventures were less lyrical and more concerned with plot and philosophical ethics, Mintegi's style has subsequently become more lyrical and introspective.

---

226   Hamilton, "Re-membering the Basque nationalist family," p. 154. In this article, Carrie Hamilton combines the literature on nationalism and gender with an oral history methodology to explore the daughter-father relationships of three female Basque ETA *(Euskadi ta Askatasuna* or Basque Country and Freedom) activists, in order to show the complex roles that parents play in transmitting nationalist values to their children.

Her most blatantly political book, *Legez kanpo* (Outside the Law), deals with the issue of a lawyer defending policemen accused of torturing prisoners, but it also has a dark detective subplot which ironically serves to lighten the mood of the book by providing the reader with a respite from the interior monologue of the narrative. The narrator is a friend of the lawyer. The reader glimpses the lawyer himself both through an occasional conversation with the friend, and through the gruesome fiction of the subplot in the guise of a novel the lawyer is writing. The detective story alternates with chapters dealing with the moral dilemma of defending Guardia Civil (the Civil Guard or Spanish paramilitary police force associated with perpetrating much social injustice and brutality) officers. The action in the detective story reveals the conflict and pain of the lawyer who is wrestling with his soul about the job he has to do. At the same time, the traditional and familiar form of the detective story provides a mental breather from the philosophical and ethical questions being addressed, even though the twisted murder story hints at the state of the lawyer's tortured soul. Thus, the character of the lawyer becomes central to the book while remaining peripheral to the linear narrative.

In her later works, *Nerea eta biok* and *Sisifo maite minez*, Mintegi moves away from more overtly political narratives and toward an intimate exploration of character. This is done gradually, since *Nerea eta biok* certainly has a strong political element, but the drama of the nationalist question and its effects on Isabel, the single mother, share the literary stage with Isabel's self-examination. In *Sisifo maite minez* self-examination takes center stage, and a political theme is virtually absent from the novel.

If we accept Deleuze and Guattari's premise that everything in a minority literature is political,[227] then Mintegi's

---

227   Gilles Deleuze and Felix Guattari, "What is Minor Literature?"

work, while evolving from purely political to principally emotional themes, actually remains very political. This point of
view confirms Mintegi's own reasons for choosing to write in
Euskara. She was raised in a Spanish-speaking home, but at
age fifteen she made a conscious decision to learn Euskara,
just as she later made a conscious (and political) decision to
write fiction in Euskara, instead of continuing with her earliest efforts that were created in Spanish. [228]

Bakhtin argues that literature and culture cannot be separated, and that culture constitutes "the indispensable context
of a literary work and of the author's position within it." [229]
Neither the work nor the author's intentions can be understood outside this context. Mintegi's novels are lucid examples of this principle at work. Autobiographical elements are
tightly woven in and out of a fictional universe that lies decep-
tively close to the cultural reality in which the author dwells.
The works themselves are imbued with greater and more varied levels of meaning when the reader is aware of how faith-
fully the author is committed to the philosophical questions
she raises. And yet the novels are fiction and the characters
are fictitious compilations of characteristics molded together

in David H. Richter, ed. *Tailing into Theory: Conflicting Views on Reading
Literature* (Boston: Bedford Books, 1994), p. 166.

228   Interview with the author. Deleuze and Guattari further claim that
in a minority literature,
...everything takes on a collective value. Indeed, precisely because talent
isn't abundant in a minor literature, there are no possibilities for an
individuated enunciation that would belong to this or that "master" and
that could be separated from a collective enunciation.
See "What is a Minor Literature?" p. 167.
In Basque literature this was true for most of the twentieth century,
but writers such as Bernardo Atxaga, Mariasun Landa, Anjel Lertxundi
and the authors studied here, are taking Basque literature to a new level.
Perhaps in another fifty years, it will no longer fall within this particular
definition of a minority literature, even though the number of speakers of Euskara will still require us to refer to the language as a minority
tongue.

229   Bakhtin, *The Dialogic Imagination*, p. 255.

to create believable people. For these reasons Mintegi's novel *Nerea eta biok* cannot be truly understood outside the context of late twentieth-century Basque culture.

Lourdes Oñederra's *Eta emakumeari sugeak esan zion* (And the Snake Said to the Woman)

The title of this novel brings to mind the story of Eve in the Garden of Eden and the battle of temptation. The book is aptly named, since the story is one of a woman who consciously places herself in the path of temptation and subsequently succumbs to it. Teresa [230] arranges with an old lover to find housing for herself and her husband for a year in Germany, while the ex-lover rents a duplex with a shared kitchen to allow himself to be close to her while she is there.

Oñederra's book shares many characteristics with early Basque novels that are now considered canonical within Basque literature. She divides the story into seasons, bringing to mind the structure of Txillardegi's *Leturiaren egunkari ezkutua* (Leturia's hidden diary). Txillardegi wrote his novel in the form of a personal diary in order to avoid the problems associated with the linguistic reality of the Basque Country in 1957, a time when speaking Basque in public could result in arrest. Faced with the predicament of writing a novel in Euskara about Basque people, Txillardegi felt he had to choose a logical place for Euskara to be used, and as such he chose the form of a personal diary.

Oñederra's book embraces the end-of-century wealth of languages in her social and cultural environment, and her seasonal breaks are enumerated in several tongues. In addition, she sprinkles German, Spanish, French, Italian, and English throughout her novel, acknowledging the multilingual real-

---

230   Oñederra's book has a female character named Teresa, and a male named Luis, just as Mintegi has in her *Nerea eta biok*. I just wanted to reassure the reader that there was no accidental mixing of characters here.

ity of Basque and European society, just as Mintegi has often done. Cixous's words again come to mind:

> But there is the language that is rich, full, vibrant with the echoes of the passengers who went from foreign language to foreign language on board their native language, tasting one and the other, writing in one, reading in others, embellishing one with the others, grafting and multiplying. [231]

However, Oñederra has her protagonist, Teresa, comment that by moving to another country, her former lover Luis avoids the need to function in multiple languages. He only needs to live in one language, albeit a foreign one, and Teresa gives the impression that she feels it must be a relief to live in a monolingual world.

From the gendered point of view, Oñederra's female protagonist is a very different woman from Urretabizkaia's single mother. The role of motherhood means nothing to this woman, Teresa, except a freedom from tedious conversations and the dreary burden of childcare. Whereas Urretabizkaia and Mintegi both grew up under Franco, Oñederra represents a generation of writers born after, or with little memory of, the dictatorship. Therefore her characters are less concerned with the political tensions that the rest of the world focuses on when it looks at the Basque Country. Teresa is a modern woman, consumed by her own emotional situation, sandwiched between her husband and her former lover. She is a woman unable to resist the temptation hinted at in the title and sleeps with them both. Oñederra's Teresa is a much more universal figure than either of the single mothers who appear in Urretabizkaia and Mintegi's works. We would not even know they were Basque except for the fact that the novel is written in Euskara and the language situation of the homeland is broached.

---

231   Cixous, *The Hélène Cixous Reader,* p. xx.

Conclusion

Basque authors write around linguistic reality by keeping their narrative confined to a personal diary, placing novels in other countries and using only Basque, or by using foreign settings but embracing non-Basque tongues to emphasize their foreignness. The three authors discussed here imbue their protagonists with daily lives lived in Euskara. In Urretabizkaia's case, living life in Euskara was a dream and a goal. In Mintegi's it was a campaign and an on-going effort. By 1999, when Onederra's novel was written, Basques who so desired were able to live in the language, but still found themselves falling back on another tongue from time to time, as when Teresa uses the expression *"Ojalá que..."* (I wish...! If only...!) and admits that she doesn't know how to say that in Euskara. She feels the lack of an equivalent subjunctive expression and yet her use of that expression demonstrates the reality of living life in a diglossic society.

For in Basque society, where one language is often favored over the other in specific situations and where Basque speakers can grow weary of the effort to find the appropriate but slippery expression in Euskara, they often just give up and say it in Spanish or French.

These novels are interesting for many reasons, but I especially find them an astounding opportunity to understand literary opinion of the language situation in the Basque Country. Furthermore, although these writers all read in Spanish and perhaps other languages as well, in addition to reading other foreign works in translation, there is a remarkable similarity in the Basque literary elements that they tend to emulate and recreate for their readers. Intimate thought, development of personal feeling, and existentialistic self-examination are all part of the literary characteristic known as Basque lyricism, for which all three authors demonstrate a great fondness.

From the Anglo-American point of view, it appears that Basque literature has turned the "show, don't tell" writer's rule upside down and made the reverse a respectable alternative. In Oñederra's novel, for example, the retarding effect of this "telling" instead of "showing" is mitigated somewhat by the urgency of second-person narration. This technique pulls the reader directly into the character and makes the thoughts and feelings a part of the reading experience. This eliminates the distance normally associated with "telling" the story instead of immersing the reader in the action. The stylistic imperatives of more mature majority languages continue to have an impact, but Basque literature is quietly molding its own narrative genre with increasing self-assuredness.

The wide gap between literary narrative and popular fiction in Basque literary circles is not unique to Basque culture. In fact, this dilemma is characteristic of small literatures in general. [232] As such, when the Basque government subsidizes literary production, publishers give preference to literary quality and high-culture content over popular genres for, as I have argued elsewhere,

> Poetry, lyric prose, existentialist self-examinations, and the sacrifice of plot for skilled language usage all maintain a high profile in works published in Basque. Those who wish to write for public consumption are marginalized and labeled bourgeois or "fluff" writers. Their works may entertain, but it is said that they have no depth and they possess little artistic merit... In this fashion they run afoul of the critical desire that Basque literature aspire to more artistic heights. [233]38

---

232   See Camartin, "Romanche, a Minor Literature," p. 74.

233

As regards gender identity in the books, Urretabizkaia's 1979 single mother is a portrait of the traditional role of women in Basque society at that point in time. Her character feels the social pressure of her condition as a single mother and spends a great deal of time evaluating her self-worth as a woman without a man. Mintegi's 1994 single mother, however, is more empowered. Instead of doubting her worth, she is angry at the male character for never growing up and avoiding his responsibilities as a parent. Yet her societal limitations are reflected in the jealousy she feels because he was able to leave these responsibilities behind whereas she could not. Indeed, she was given no choice in the matter and once her first child was born, her fate was sealed. She would never be free again. Oñederra's Teresa, on the other hand, has no children. She even complains about the general lack of intelligent conversation from any parent in a social situation. By 1999 a woman (at least, in a novel) could not only remain childless but could resent the presence and importance of children in the lives of her friends.

Although the authors are only separated by eleven years in age (Urretabizkaia was born in 1947, Mintegi in 1955, and Oñederra in 1958), their works present us with differences that feel not only distinctly generational but are most likely also derived from their varied experiences growing up in Basque culture at slightly different times. From an outsider's perspective, however, all three seem to avoid any overtly feminist sentiments. However, this in itself may be a message for the reader.

Afterword

Can you inhale the past on a sea breeze? That was the question that plagued me as I strolled among the tamarind trees on the promenade in Donostia. I watched the grandmothers strolling with their friends, wearing the uniform of their generation, flat-soled shoes, straight skirts, blouses and cardigans in the earth tones that were de rigueur that year. Could the memories of these women be changing who I was? Or was I being silly to think I could feel the past of an entire people weighing heavily in the air I was breathing?

They looked so peaceful and calm, straight-backed ladies speaking a language I was working hard to learn. I'd been studying it for thirteen years at that point, and as the months passed, my fluency level improved. I could do radio interviews and television guest spots in Euskara, much to the delight of my teachers, but I often felt like Mark Twain's dancing dog. It wasn't so much that I danced well. It was just a marvel that I danced at all. I wasn't Basque. I had no Basque ancestors. And technically I learned to speak the language in the United States. My skills were sufficient to carry me to Euskal Herria on a quest for material for a doctorate in Basque Studies, but people kept asking me, "Why? Why are you here?"

These women who marched slowly along the promenade asked the question with their eyes. They saw me coming from a long way off, with my Anglo heritage, my pale blue eyes, and my glow-in-the-dark skin. Most assumed I was British. Even little children would stop me and ask, "Inglesa?" "English?" Meaning my nationality, not my language. After a while I began nodding, yes, English. Why not? All my ancestors came from the British Isles, and even the Danish corner of the family had its representative in Hamlet, didn't it? Sure. English. That's me. And it was easier than contradicting the evidence with explanations.

The women saw me coming, and their eyes would swoop toward me, like the gulls over the bay swooping toward a fish. *Kanpokoa.* "Outsider." *Herbestekoa.* "Foreigner." And the question would be written in their eyebrows, in the crinkle of a forehead, the angle of a mouth or the jut of a chin. *Zergatik zaude hemen?* "Why are you here?"

At first, it bothered me. It was unsettling, to have all these eyes collaborate in their scrutiny, to have all these foreheads posing silent questions. Sometimes I looked back and smiled. The American armor. Smile, smile, smile. What a shock to learn that some other cultures considered us childlike and foolish because we smile so much. I wondered if Basque-Americans ever had to explain to their European relatives that smiling is something we are taught to do from infancy, especially if we are women. "Smile, sweetie!" "Where's your smile?" "Smiles make fewer wrinkles than frowns." "Service with a smile." And if we're too tired to smile, we can wear a smiley button or paste on a smiley bumper sticker.

So I would look back and smile, and they would look away. Or they would frown harder and try to stare the smile off my face. If I were tired, I would just keep my eyes front and pay no attention to the stares. But they were there, waiting for me, if I let down my guard.

As I learned more about the history of the Basque people, the stares bothered me less and less. Especially the stares of these grandmothers, these sturdy women who braced their families against the daily onslaught of life under Franco. Many of them were children during the Spanish Civil War. Their young lives were scarred by bombing raids and firing squads and streets full of soldiers. And after the Civil War came the hunger and the humiliation, as Spain reeled under the economic devastation caused by its internal struggles and Franco garrisoned two-thirds of his Guardia Civil, the national police force, inside the borders of the Basque provinces.

What did they have to smile about back then? How many friends did they see off at the docks when compassionate nations opened their doors and invited the Basques to send their children to safe havens for the duration of the war? And how many friends did they never see again, when World War II erupted before the Spanish Civil War children could be returned to their families? Pockets of Basques grew to maturity in Mexico, Argentina, Great Britain, Canada, and the Soviet Union. They were supposed to spend a few months abroad, then return home when the war was over. But for them and for the children who remained in the Basque Country, it must have felt like the war would never end. Their entire childhood was lived in the shadow of war.

And those shadows still haunted the faces of the grandmothers on the promenade. The sun was shining, and perfect white puffs of cloud decorated the autumn blue sky. Fishing boats painted in primary colors bobbed on the waves like Brobdingnagian bathtub toys, just far enough away to feed the illusion that no humans sat on the bridge or worked on the decks. The soft ocher sandstone of the city circled La Concha with golden arms. The buildings were only eight stories high. No skyscrapers darkened the promenade. And yet these Basque grandmothers walked in shadow.

Can you inhale the past in the souring dampness of six-hundred-year-old stones? I walked alone through the artificial gray canyons of the Siete Calles neighborhood of Bilbao and felt the history of the city pressing in on me from all sides. The narrow cobbled streets, the balconies overhanging here and there, and the thick ill-fitting ancient doors spoke of the distant past, while more recently installed shop windows displayed Nikes and Macs and Sony and IBM.

New and old clashed loudly as trucks and workmen jammed into the Plaza Nueva (which wasn't new at all) to put up decorations for the coming festival. Young and old clashed as adolescent girls shopped and giggled through the Siete Calles while their carefully coiffed grandmothers and stoop-shouldered great-grandmothers moved somberly from bread store to fishmonger to poulterer's. A sudden downpour sent everyone scurrying for shelter in the deep doorways, huddled together, shoulder to shoulder but silent and separate. Everyone waited for the rain to let up. A few brave souls opened their umbrellas and trudged on, forced to brave the weather by work schedules or social assignations. I watched the waters swirl and roll along the stone gutter in the middle of the cobbled street, and I wondered if the rain would wash the smell of age away.

It didn't.

Can you inhale the past in the sun-warmed salty air of a narrow alley in the old part of Algorta? The walls of the houses are so close together you could touch one with your fingertips and reach across to touch another with the other hand. When these houses were built, this was not an alley, but a street. There were no cars that needed to be parked in front of the house. The street needed to be wide enough to let people walk through. Wide enough to let a burro turn around. And it didn't need to be flat, either. Stairs were built into the passage every few yards to make it easier to go up and down the hill. I stood in the sunshine at a pre-automotive intersection. Go right and down the steps to the beach. Go left and up the passageway toward the top of the hill. The windows in the houses have flower boxes, and splashes of pink and vermilion and green adorn the whitewashed walls.

I chose up.

I walked past a small paved recess between the entries to two different houses. A family had built a patio-in-miniature there, and someone's grandmother was hanging out the laundry on a revolving clothesline. She was not dressed for promenading, just for ordinary housework. She wore a white sleeveless frock with little blue flowers all over it. A delicate cream-colored slip hung about her calves, revealed when she reached up to hang a stocking or a brassiere.

My passing surprised her, and she looked startled. Then she blushed and smiled, covering her mouth for a moment in a universal language that said, "I didn't expect anyone to see me hanging out my undies!" I smiled back, happy to know that women can still share some things without speaking a word.

I kept climbing. The narrow street wound to the right and grew even narrower. My American sensibilities made me feel like an intruder. If I climbed any higher, I would be so close to windows and doors that I might inadvertently peep through and witness some private part of a life that wasn't mine. That made me uncomfortable, so I stopped. Just one photograph, and then I'd go back down. I lifted my camera, and a small black dog emerged from a cross street every bit as narrow as the one I was on. It stood there, only thirty feet away but higher than my head. That was the perfect photograph for the dog-loving American tourist.

I walked back down the same way I'd come, but the grandmother with the cream-colored slip had finished her chore and gone back inside. There was nothing of the past on this tiny patio. The air was redolent with fabric softener.

These houses belonged to fisherfolk when they were first built, and at the bottom of the steps was a small park where I found a statue of a female fishmonger. She stood forever silent, waiting patiently no matter what the weather, a basket of fish on her head. Another photograph for the tourist, for that was how I felt in that neighborhood. After years of studying the language and the culture, I was reduced to surface tourism, capturing images of a different way of life on film, to develop at home and wonder what it was like to grow old in one of those tidy little dwellings on the stepping-stone street. I breathed deeply, trying to catch some faint fishy odor, but there was nothing save the clean sea breeze and the myriad histories of the women of the Basque Country.

— Linda White

Acknowledgments

Publication of this volume was made possible by funding from the Basque Government, in collaboration with the Ministry of Education, Universities and Research, the Ministry of Culture, and the Secretary General of Foreign Affairs.

In addition, some funding was provided by members of and donors to the Consortium for the Study of Basque Women (1997–2002).

Made in the USA
Middletown, DE
25 March 2022

63151866R00137